SEXUALITY, MANHOOD, & OTHER STORIES

BENT

J. ADAMS

ISBN: 979-8-9856972-0-9

Interior design by Booknook.biz.

"Only the human mind invents categories and tries to force facts into separated pigeon-holes. The living world is a continuum in each and every one of its aspects."

—Alfred C. Kinsey, *Sexual Behavior in the Human Male*

CONTENTS

I. QUALIFICATIONS

My twenty-seventh birthday was just around the corner, and I thought it might be time to mix things up a bit. My relationships with women hadn't turned out so well, and even though I'd identified the pattern—falling for, sleeping with, and then bailing on a woman after months and more of intense coupling—I'd been unable to stop repeating it. After the last time, I swore I wouldn't be responsible for any more endings, but there I was, in another relationship, and feeling itchy again.

If the sex hadn't been good that would've been one thing. Presumably, a light bulb would've gone off about seven girlfriends back. But when I considered past breakups and the time spent between the sheets leading up to them, the best I could come up with was: Generally effortless. Always fun. Plentiful. My only regret was that no matter how good it got, it was never enough to prevent the inevitable, only prolong it.

It wasn't just that I'd suddenly remember I didn't want to be tied down after having previously given every indication that I did. It was that I'd promptly forget it all over again when taking up with someone new. Pretty sneaky. But even if I had considered it, it wouldn't have been too much of a stretch to tell myself It'll Be Different This Time because one issue I never seemed to have was falling for the same type of woman. Each was so totally her own that I was having a hard time coming up with anything they had in common besides the fact that they were women. Women who had all reached the conclusion I was an asshole.

What I needed was another explanation for my behavior, and the more I thought about it, the more I'd begun to warm to the idea that I might be gay. Not quite so much that I personally felt like celebrating, but if it were revealed to be true, then at least my previous girlfriends should be able to. "No, it wasn't us. It was him all along. And he wasn't really being an asshole, he was just confused, poor thing." The only problem was being gay wasn't supposed to be something you just signed up for and I wasn't sure I qualified.

CONNECTICUT

As far as I could tell, I didn't have any memories of being physically attracted to guys growing up. Racking my brain for guys who could even be considered potential candidates, I could only come up with two. Peter was the first adult to insist I use his given name; he was close friends with my parents and I adored him. He'd toss me in the air every time I saw him. He taught me card tricks, gave me my first gyroscope. With his wife, Danielle, he took his sailboat around the world and always had great adventures to share. He drowned in a boating accident. I just didn't think there was any drama there beyond that.

The other guy was a regular at the pool I swam at in the summer. A teenager, probably an older teen. On his shoulders, I felt near invincible. Defending our chickenfighting title, or rising up out of the water with him holding tight to my ankles, steadying me before I was ready to jump. When he threw me across the pool, I'd keep circling back for more. Until I'd finally get the message he'd had enough and swim off to be with my friends. I was still just as excited to see him the next time he showed up at the pool, but it was hard to believe there was much going on besides a desire for more horseplay.

With guys my own age, it felt like much of the same thing. Whether it was the kid I played chase with in the basement where things got a little grabby if you got caught. Or fooling around with my teammates after swim practice. Everything from having peeing contests in the shower to giving each other rat tails—twisted-up towels that left crazy red marks on bare skin when you snapped them just right—while we were trying to get changed.

It all seemed pretty innocent, but worth taking a peek at, I think, to remind myself that my lack of physical attraction toward guys hadn't been the result of my not having had the chance to have it. I was hardly a shut-in. Participating in sports year-round meant I spent a fair bit of time in the locker room, and there'd been lots of opportunities to feel the discomfort that gay men talk about feeling in there when they were younger. But I didn't feel it, either before or after pubic hair.

If I was looking for something to start my resume with, I'd need to look elsewhere.

The *Playgirl* incident should've been a contender because, well, I looked at a *Playgirl* and felt weird about it. But with the way that reading exercise turned out, I doubted it was going to do much to help build my case.

That year, the Junior Nationals were being held in Pittsburgh and we were doing our best not to feel extraordinarily ripped off because the year before they'd been in Hawaii. I'd already been to the pool to practice, and was back hanging in the hotel gift shop with the Armstrong brothers when they called me over to check out this magazine they were half surreptitiously looking through. They were giggling like mad, but I was less than amused when they showed me the picture of some guy with a dick the size of Manhattan. What I remember thinking was not the Armstrong brothers are gay, or I'm gay for doing a triple-take here, but *Oh man, my little willy I just washed in the shower is never gonna cut it.* And *How does he get his to stand at attention like that?* And *Why has nobody told me this is what I'm up against?* Basically, this is bullshit.

"It's gotta be fake," we all agreed.[1]

If the average age a gay man first becomes aware of his sexuality is, indeed, ten,[2] then it seemed like I'd just missed the boat. Or at least the first launch. Even after having been presented with relevant material, I still wasn't able to conjure a sexual thought about a man. What I saw was competition. And even though I wasn't in the habit of losing those, either in or out of the pool, it wasn't the first time I felt like I might've gotten the short end of the stick.

While my guy-ness was about average compared with my teammates, the guys I went to school with, it was a different story in the neighborhood where I grew up. I worried I wasn't tough enough. A fear that would only have been more keenly felt if I'd realized the guys I did consider tough would've been snacked on by even tougher kids in other neighborhoods. This was not quite suburban Connecticut, after all, where horse fencing and barns dotted the landscape and pretty much everything backed up to forest.

---

[1] It turns out *Playgirl* wasn't generally into showing fully erect penises, so they had the guy get hard and then shot him coming down from there (which couldn't have been an easy feat for either the model to maintain or the cameraman to capture as that's a pretty quick transition). Having said that, it would appear we got lucky with our issue (and I got lucky on eBay). Looking at it now, I suppose I shouldn't be surprised not to see anything threatening. And yet, I can tell how a number of the shots would have represented a significant change from what we'd all seen in the men's locker room, since even a modestly engorged penis would've been a bit of a shock. https://www.esquire.com/entertainment/a55592/playgirl-magazine-history/

[2] https://www.pewsocialtrends.org/2013/06/13/chapter-3-the-coming-out-experience/

Summertime, mostly, we'd all be out running around on Fog Wood Road, tons of us it always seemed, only called in for dinner and then back out again until dark, or after dark if we were playing Ghost in the Graveyard. The biggest strike against me was that during the day when the genders sometimes divided up, I liked hanging out with the girls as much as the guys. The fact that I was equally happy playing school as playing football was cause for suspicion. Girl By Association might have been the charge, which was somehow considered about the worst thing a guy could be at the time. I took shit for it, didn't like taking shit for it, but was still stubborn enough to play with whoever I wanted to on any given day. For a while, anyway.

Another strike against me was my age. Whether I'd just turned seven or nine or eleven, I'd always be the second youngest boy in the neighborhood, and that meant I didn't carry any clout and was expected to fall in line. The only boy younger than me—by a year—was a great kid. The one I played chase with in my basement, in fact. I can't remember a bad time when the two of us hung out together, but when our unofficial neighborhood bully joined us, he would always pit us against each other. I had a basically benign younger sister and this other boy had a houseful of older brothers that used to whale on him pretty regularly, and it took me a while to figure out how to fight back rather than cry. A lesson he'd learned long before me. Half the tears came from being too wimpy, and the other half, I think, just general frustration that we could be turned on one another so easily.

This is the kind of crap you go through as a guy. I remember the first time I got the upper hand fighting and the bully threw me a compliment. Here was my actual friend (when the bully wasn't around), sobbing, and I'm feeling, not in any way proud of myself, but relieved it's not me. The takeaway seemed obvious—the best way to get respect was to make sure you came out on top. But it was a narrow view of the world—this zero-sum game between guys, where it seemed like there always had to be a winner and a loser—and my sense that the girls might be onto something with the way they collaborated more had taken the real hit.

Still, the overall experience of fighting toughened me up some, and it's hard not to see the positive in that. I didn't need to be getting upset about every scratch or bruise or even injury. So I owe the bully for that. Although I'd like to think there's about a hundred better ways that it could have been brought out in me.

Like all bullies, this bully was more than just a bully. He had a name (which I remember well). He was a number of years older (and, of course, had an older brother). And last I heard, he'd ended up in jail. But at times he could be super cool to hang out with, and it is to him I owe my first real taste in music. He used to blast Yes's "Roundabout" on his speakers, over and over, telling me to pay particular attention to the guitar intro. To my house, he brought *Led Zeppelin IV*, *Abbey Road*. If I really believed musical taste was reflective of sexuality, then the first two albums I bought for myself could've offered some clues: Boston's *Boston*. And Donna Summer's *Greatest Hits Vol. 1 and 2*.

But I bought the Boston first.

All my dreams I remember growing up were about girls, usually saving them from one predicament or another. Jen C. (back when every third girl was named Jennifer) was a regular. The dreams were intense—I'd still be clinging to the remnants of them the next morning at school, feeling extra protective toward a girl who couldn't possibly understand where my feelings were coming from—but you'd be hard pressed to call them sexual in nature. Nothing was, really, until sixth grade. And even then, it was all kissing and "she likes you" and "look who's wearing a training bra." Listening to the sexuality talk at school, I had a feeling it was a long way off, although the teachers were smart—getting ahead of it—because it wasn't long after that I began to realize what they were talking about.

I remember the first time I accidentally jerked off and thought the world had just come to an end in the best possible way. All this fun to be had in my own bedroom? Unbelievable. So that became a thing, and not long afterward, the even messier night version—the "nocturnal emissions" I'd been warned about. Between the two, this meant I was sending my underwear down to the laundry basket in all kinds of condition, and my mom must have had a talk with my dad 'cause there he was one day pressing me about it. I believe it was the one time in my life I ever lied to my father. Preposterously claiming I didn't know anything about it (my parents had just separated, and I was thinking, *You don't even live here anymore, you've got no right to talk to me about this stuff*). But I did handle my jizz differently after that.

At first, I was just wanking because it felt great, not focused on anything but doing it. I wasn't fantasizing about anyone or anything. I mean, I wouldn't have even thought to think of anything else, it felt so good on its own. But eventually I graduated to girly magazines that my buddies and I had swiped.

Now, here was something I might be able to use. Working my way through my stash, there was maybe a sense of following protocol, like somewhere along the way I'd picked up the idea that this was the proper way to be handling myself. And even though I'd develop a greater appreciation for The Wide World of Tits a bit later, once I'd made contact, at the time I remember thinking, *What's the big deal, I've seen my mom's plenty of times.* Still, there was genuine interest and curiosity. My favorite spread was of a woman with her fingers inside, spreading her lips and suggesting an entire world that merited exploring. Probably it was the newness of it. Hidden treasure and all that. Fortunately, this was not something my mom had put on display before.

I stuck that poster of Heather "by the hot tub" Locklear up on my wall, but even then I recognized it as a bit of a sham, thinking I was into it, but not as much as I thought I should be. My most alpha friend, John D. (back when every third guy was named John), talked about girls' bodies constantly, and I knew for a fact that I didn't have that same level of interest. I suppose there was an opportunity to question my sexuality here, but I didn't take it, as John stood out compared not just to me, but to the rest of our friends, as being a little excessive in his enthusiasm for the female form. Still, the two of us competed in a number of areas, and this was one where I suspected he had the upper hand.[3]

---

[3] What *did* get me off about that poster? The way Ms. Locklear pulled that pink bikini strap away from her hip. If I'd been able to articulate the reason why— that it was the suggestion of sex that I was drawn toward, that it didn't really matter who was in the picture, or what, exactly, her body looked like—that would've made me a pretty savvy thirteen-year-old. One who might have guessed that if he'd seen that *Playgirl* spread a couple years later and something sexual had been happening in the picture rather than simply "Guy and His Shlong," maybe there would've been a reaction.

So what does it mean to walk into a school dance and be the first guy in your group to point out the best-looking gal in the room? Well, today, obviously, it means you're a sexist, primitive toad, but back in my day it could mean a lot of things, all of them generally conveyed in one of two ways: either with a gesture—a hit on your buddy's shoulder and a quick nod of your chin— or a comment. Let's go with the comment.

"Hey man, look over there in the corner. She's hot." Guy Number 1 says this while being fully and genuinely focused on the gal in the corner. He'll be thinking to himself, *Hey, the rest of you guys are cool and everything, but what I'd really like to be able to do is shake you off as soon as possible and get with her.* He'll be working on a plan to end up near enough to her so he can make his move. He will almost certainly follow through and talk with her (unless he sees someone he considers better-looking on the way over). If things go well, and the girl is interested, he will get her number or go somewhere with her. He's a Closer.

"Hey, man, look over there in the corner. She's hot." Guy Number 2 believes he's the poor man's version of Guy Number 1 and he's right. His comment is some percentage about the girl and the rest for the guys he's with. He's not running a plan through in his mind to get over there, but part of him would be happy if they bumped into one another. Or, better, if she came up to him. He'd still be nervous talking to her. In fact, he's not really sure he wants her to come up to him at all. He's a bit of a Waffler, but ultimately persuadable.

"Hey, man, look over there in the corner. She's hot." Guy Number 3—the Friendster—says this all the time. It's a throwaway comment, made in the same way he'd point out a good play watching football. ("Hey, man, did you see that pass?

Incredible.") It doesn't mean he's queer; it just means he doesn't have nearly the same interest as Guy Number 1 and less even than Guy Number 2. He'd just as soon make his comment, check the chick box (I'm not queer) and then go hang out with his buddies, which is why he really wants to be there.

This is just for illustrative purposes, of course. No matter what your age, you don't necessarily behave the same every single night you go out. At least, I didn't. To the extent I pointed girls out, I generally fell somewhere between guys number 2 and 3, but even when I found someone really attractive, I was only playing along. Because I almost always had a girlfriend and wasn't the type to think seriously about messing around on the side.

I remember working my way around the bases with my seventh-through-tenth-grade girlfriend. She was blonde and her name was the same as one of the Brady girls, I'll let you guess which one. I was at this Catholic school for boys where everyone was some version of smart; I wasn't the strongest entry by a long shot. They gave us a lot of freedom in between demanding classes and sometimes I'd end up with these back-to-back free periods. I imagine I was supposed to be somewhere (like the library? I think we had one) but it wasn't like anyone checked up on you. My girlfriend lived not far from the school, her (single) mom worked, and she would stay home from time to time with minor colds on days that matched my schedule. That meant in the middle of the school day I could walk over there and get some couch time. An insanely good setup.

Anyway, the day I rounded third base with her was a revelation. I went back to school a new man. Smelling my finger along the way, during class, even taking a moment for reflection in the restroom. I can still see me standing there in front of the sink trying to get in one last sniff, and then thinking, *Nope, not gonna wash today.*

This girl would become the first person I ever slept with, but the romance ran into a pretty big stumbling block when I ended up moving a thousand miles away.

GEORGIA

So there I was midway through my sophomore year and—faced with the prospect of transferring from a private school to a public one in the Deep South—I was expecting nothing but trouble. My mom had made it clear we couldn't afford Connecticut anymore, and even though I'd protested that there was surely lower income housing to be found in the state, the time for arguing that point or any other had ended. We had a goodbye party the night before I left, back in the endless woods behind my house, and I remember my friends sitting around the campfire attempting these really awful Southern accents, giving me a hard time about how I'd soon be chewing tobacco and driving a tractor (both things I ended up doing but not in Georgia). Underneath it all, though, was some real sadness. On the way down the coast, I alternated between dry heaving and throwing up at the various rest stops, and while in the car, curled up with my sleeping bag and a Stephen King book, pretending nothing important was happening.

Reality caught up soon enough. First day at the new school, and they had one of the Student Council stars showing me around, my locker and building layout and such. Near the end of the tour, he stopped and looked around the hallway, then lowered his voice all confidential like and said to me, "Listen, you better not wear that jean jacket around here or people will think you're into drugs." Naturally, I sensed right then I'd be needing to get into drugs to deal with these Student Council types.

While I was busy plotting my return to the Northeast for college and wondering if I could make it through the next two and a half years without having to speak to anyone, along came this group of coolish misfits and when they offered to take me under their wing, I wasn't inspired to put up a fight (also, one of them started giving me a ride to school in the mornings, so there was that).

One guy in this group was an actor. He'd already had a major role in a minor film, which I found impressive, and he was sarcastic as hell, which I loved. Today, I probably wouldn't have much trouble figuring out he was gay, but back then you tended not to think anyone was *really* gay. In the school, and possibly on the planet. You could call someone a fag or be called a fag. You could note feminine behaviors in guys (or masculine ones in girls), but you didn't really have it in your mind that some guy was actually sucking some other guy's dick in the boys' bathroom (unless you were the one doing the sucking or getting sucked, in which case you were a few steps ahead of the rest of us).

I'd been over to this actor guy's house once or twice to listen to music, play Risk or whatever board game was lying around. Uneventful hang out time. Then one day I stayed home from school and the guy dropped by my house with a Get Well card. A little over the top, I thought, I was just a little under the weather and didn't feel like going in, but he didn't know that.

Maybe it was just an extension of that whole Southern hospitality thing. Anyway, the printed part of the card said your standard get well stuff, but on the blank side there was a handwritten message written in code. He'd already left when I opened it, and being curious, I set out to crack it. It wasn't that hard, so I didn't have too long to let my fears build up, but whatever ones were there were quickly realized. He'd written, "I love you," along with some other gushing stuff I don't exactly remember. I was instantly twisted up inside.

Here's where I get uncool and it won't be the last time. I cut him off. Immediately and forever. And you have to understand, it still wasn't the case that I was thinking he was really interested in me in any sort of sexual way. I remembered no X or even PG rated images in my mind. Just the fact that another guy thought he loved me and I was wigged out. Pathetic, I know, but that's where I was.

I think I did something ridiculous like make sure the card was torn to shreds before escorting it to the main trash can outside, not being satisfied with the one in my room. Throwing away the evidence but not the memory. Like what made this guy possibly think I could be like that? And deep down inside, I thought—couldn't help but think—maybe there's something.

That there can be such angst as a result of someone of the same gender revealing they love you is difficult to justify. Especially when you've got to know on some level that the same things that are going to make you attractive to one gender are just as likely to make you attractive to another. You should be able to treat it like any other crush—you're either into it or you're not—but it feels like there's more on the line, and you're prone to question yourself. Is there something you're doing, have done, something about you? When I spoke with the older classmate who'd been giving me the ride to school about what had happened—a kind of den mother for the group and the one person I thought I could confide in about why I wouldn't be hanging out anymore—she said, "I told him he was wasting his time." My first reaction was *Wait, you* knew *about this?* quickly followed by *Okay, glad you didn't think I was leading him on.*

Maybe in part because of this discussion, I didn't feel the need to compensate for what'd happened by changing myself. I didn't lower my voice an octave, or walk taller, or join the football team to try to highlight how I wasn't the type. Instead, I settled in with a new group of friends who were decidedly non-macho like me, and yet, at the same time, were guy's guys by most any definition.

In common, we shared stepdads or abusive dads or drunk dads or distant dads—emotionally—or, in my case, just living far away. To varying degrees we were on our own when it came to figuring out what manhood meant, and as best as I can tell, we learned to build on our various chunks of masculinity from one another. Unconsciously. Just by hanging out so much. Whether it was at the river drinking beer or fixing cars and drinking beer or playing poker and drinking beer (pretty much every activity that could conceivably be paired with beer drinking was), there wasn't a lot of chest thumping associated with the activities, and that applied whether our equally laid-back girlfriends were with us or not. Sure, we had part-time jobs and made our marks at school when we needed to, but otherwise our time together passed pretty unremarkably.

I'd be surprised to learn that any one of us was questioning anyone else's sexuality. I know I never did. And as to what anyone else may have questioned about themselves, I couldn't say. But when it comes to the elusive purity of "straightness," all it takes is one chink in the armor to have doubts, and I sustained what I thought was a pretty significant one my junior year.

It cracks me up now because the whole thing seems so innocent in the context of what happened later (or any context, really), but at the time, it was cause for alarm. So there was this older group of guys and gals that we often tied in with, cooler than us for at least the reason of being seniors, and the craziest of the cool was this one guy named Charlie. He was quick to offer a hand up, a smile, would do or say anything for a laugh, but the laugh was rarely at anyone else's expense and that was probably my favorite thing about him. I was always happy to see him at parties or around town, and initially felt the same way when he showed up in one of my dreams.

In it, the two of us were standing around some playground, shooting the shit, hands in our pockets. About an arm's length from one another. And then at a certain point we stopped talking, one of us maybe kicked at the dirt, before we finally reached out to one another. Held each other in a bear hug for a good while, and I woke up with a hard-on and freaked. Can you imagine? Scandalous. But this was before I knew about erections and REM sleep (that sixth grade sex ed course could've used an upgrade) and also before I fully realized what an idiot I was being around the subject, so I was literally sweating with fear that this meant I was homo bound. It wasn't just that the dream had been generated by me. Or even the fact that it represented the first thought I'd had about a guy in seventeen years that resembled something sexual. The thing I couldn't shake when I woke up was the memory of how good it had felt to hold—and be held by—the guy, and the recognition that there was some longing to get back to that.

Charlie was perfectly primed for high school in many ways, but even my emotionally diminutive teenage brain was able to guess from the occasional stray comment or careless action with himself that somewhere in there he was hurting. I was hurting at the time myself—family stuff, mostly—but I wanted to believe I could handle it on my own and I think Charlie ran his life the same way. Meaning, at a cost. We probably both could've used that hug.

When my friends and I went up to visit Charlie his freshman year at Clemson, I can't say I was all that surprised to see he was already in trouble. That very afternoon he'd taken his knife, heated it, then burned it directly into his forearm, twice, making the shape of a cross. It was a mess, and even though he tried to brush it off as he unwrapped the bandages to show us ("Yeah, I'm nuts but kinda neat, right?"), I remember wincing inside and it wasn't because of being squeamish at the sight of raw skin.

If there was no longing left from that dream, there was at least a memory of longing. A desire briefly lit up for—and by—me. To reach out and connect more intimately with another guy. To find something healing in that connection. That sounded promising, but I could just picture myself walking into an interview with Gay Inc. and being asked why I wanted the position. "Well, I had this dream once," wasn't likely to go over very well. Especially when you considered no one had even gotten naked in it. Still, it was at least as strong as anything else I had going for me at the moment, so you can be sure I kept it, leaving me with a list of potential qualifications that looked something like:

1. Hung out with girls as much as guys at an age when that wasn't considered appropriate.
2. Bought a Donna Summer album.
3. Sensed I should've been more overwhelmed by women's bodies.
4. Got a love note from another guy and
5. Had an unsettling dream.

There was also this: Over the course of my adolescence, I remember catching very occasional references to gay people in the media. Probably not a movie, but a book, a couple of articles. A magazine cover comes to mind. These references weren't enough to remove gay people from their ultimately hypothetical status, but they caught my attention. It wasn't so much a question of what my reaction contained (it was mixed), but the fact that I'd had a reaction in the first place. I distinctly remember wanting it to be easy. Like, *Oh look, gay people are having a revolution*, just more interesting information about the world, like, *Oh look, there's an uprising in Zimbabwe.* But it didn't go like that.

If I was reading a sentence about a quick brown fox, I didn't want it to be any different than if it was a gay brown fox jumping over that lazy dog, but I would feel just the slightest bit of a catch when I came across the word *gay* and I didn't like it. What, exactly, was I getting caught on? Not like I would've had any way of knowing what other guys were thinking when they encountered such passages—maybe they weren't sailing through either—and it wasn't like I would have asked. I suppose I could've been more curious about it rather than simply brushing it off—maybe that would've led to something helpful—but it just didn't seem like the most pressing question of my adolescence.

What did seem important was that I was going off to college, and for the most part, feeling good about my prospects. Yes, a few questionable things had happened. And maybe there were guys out there who'd had fewer or even none of my type of experiences, but it was hard to believe that mine were that far out of line for your average American guy. Mostly, my mind was occupied with trying to figure out women, and how I was acting around them.

I'd had two serious girlfriends in Georgia, completely different from one another, but my feeling for both of them had been equally strong. Each time, I was sure I was in love—as sure as a teenager can be, anyway—and what confused me (not to mention the women), was how that intensity of feeling ended up turning back on itself. It was like the better it was between us, the better it continued to get, until things seemed so good that I could picture settling down and even having a family with them. That was right when I'd bail. It happened seemingly overnight, like a switch had been flipped, and I didn't feel like I was in control of the switch. Still, I didn't consider it part of some larger problem. *I'm just too young for this sort of thing,* I'd tell myself, *that's all.*

That theory had been steadily losing credibility, of course. To the point where I found myself on the cusp of my twenty-seventh birthday and re-evaluating all my interactions along the way. But I was trying to stay focused, so I pressed on to a high school tie-in that brought me around to men again, specifically to an old boss of mine.

The summer I turned fifteen, I lived with my dad and worked at a factory in Bridgeport. It was the best job. I was the only teenager, the only *gringo*, and the guys teasing me about these facts only went so far, with the rest filled in by them treating me far too well (Tito, where are you now?). It was just us down on the factory floor or in the freight elevator, moving boxes, stacking them, loading trucks, with the occasional clipboard-carrying, instruction-changing person materializing from the office world above.

But I was up in the office every two weeks to collect my paycheck, where I'd sometimes see my boss, a business associate and friend of my father's who'd gotten me the job. He was always pleasant, asking me how things were going. Just basic banter except for this one time when he told me to step outside and then asked me how things were going *really*.

My parents were mired in a hella divorce, one so bad it was still being referred to a decade later in legal circles as an example of what not to do in the courtroom, but I didn't know this at the time. I just knew my heart was broken. And because I had only recently begun construction on the wall I was to eventually build around it, and because the guy already knew something about what was going on from my father—I didn't have to explain everything—and because I had a shit ton of unexpressed feelings, having never opened up to my friends beyond the occasional cynical comment, I let 'em rip. I not only said it sucked but proceeded to count the ways it sucked. The more I said, the more I wanted to say, and it took quite a while before I'd finally exhausted myself.

My boss listened carefully. Rarely interrupting, asking the occasional pertinent question. And then, near the end, he made me an offer. He said if I wanted, he would talk to my dad about my coming to stay with him and his wife until the steam blew off. I remember thinking I would've taken him up on it in a second—*a second.* I was so desperate, I would've stayed with pretty much anyone who wasn't my mom or dad at that point. But even though he did bring it up with my father, I knew the suggestion wouldn't go anywhere, and it didn't (and it's a good thing because the steam never blew off and I might still be living with him).

Anyway, all it took was this one day for me to mark my boss as an ally. So years later when I was passing through Connecticut on the way down from college and my dad told me the guy wanted to grab a bite to eat with me, I said sure. My dad then asked if I was sure I was sure, and when I looked at him funny, he said there was something I needed to know. I was surprised by the new information, but said I'd still go.

The first part of the meal was about how grown up I'd become and all that, me telling my old boss about college. The second part was him telling me he didn't know if I'd heard but he'd just left his wife; he'd fallen in love with another man. This was the part my dad had already told me. In fact, my boss said, the guy looked a lot like me. This was the part my dad hadn't. *Jesus.*

What is wrong with me, was all I could think. *Like what did I do to merit this turn in the conversation?* I hadn't even fully processed the offer to come live with him from years earlier as being, unfairly or not, more creepy than generous, and already I was jonesing to get out of there. Still, I tried to keep my cool, asking polite questions, and doing my best to listen with all the patience he'd once given me when I'd been the one wanting to talk. Eventually, he got around to his central thesis, which was that the difference between sex with his male lover and sex with his (soon to be) ex-wife was the difference between a lamp being turned on high and low. *Was this an example of what people meant when they talked about gay recruiting?*

There was no way I could accuse my dad of a setup since he'd given me the big reveal in advance, but I wondered if he'd had his own doubts about me. I had agreed to meet up with the guy, after all, and maybe he took that as curiosity. As a parent, myself, I can say this kind of thing does cross your mind. Like your oldest boy's letting some seriously attractive coeds paint his fingernails in the living room and does that make him comfortable with his masculinity and willing to leverage that comfort to increase his odds of getting a date, or is he really into that fingernail polish? (Or, nowadays, it seems like, both.) Anyway, when I followed up with my dad afterward, we had a good talk. Both of us doing our best to be openminded, modern men, neither of us mentioning any potential resemblance between me and the lover. Sure, we said, it had to have been tough on the wife, but hopefully they'd all be happier in the long run.

I can't say I was feeling as nonchalant about it as I'd led my dad to believe, but looking at it again, it wasn't clear why I should've been getting that stirred up. So I'd had a relationship with another guy who turned out to be gay. So what? Like the one back in high school that'd ended with the PS I Love You card, this didn't seem like a case where I'd be able to turn another man's sexuality into a referendum on my own. Which meant I wouldn't be getting much credit for the association.

This idea of setting up an interview with Gay Inc. was looking increasingly problematic. But what was I supposed to do? I was already in the office, and even though I'd been squirming in my chair half the time, the guy conducting it hadn't made me feel like I had no business being there. He might have even shown some interest in a couple of points along the way. But he'd also stifled a yawn, and if I wasn't mistaken, he was moments away from telling me how nice it was to meet me, that he had all my materials, and would be sure to be in touch if anything opened up.

And even though I really didn't want to talk about it, I realized that if I was being serious—*Do you want this job or not?* —then I had better hurry up and get all my cards on the table before it was too late.

I was on my way back up to college, staying with my dad, and hanging out with one of my best friends from prep school who I usually managed to see while visiting. Even though we'd been in the same class, the guy was a year older than me, and I had always considered him, by prep boy standards, the toughest kid in school. Italian, sounding like he'd accidentally stumbled in from the Bronx to Connecticut's suburbs, where he consequently called bullshit on pretty much everything and everyone. Honest, loyal. Would meet anyone's definition of a good friend.

From the beginning, I suspected he was a better person than I was, and, unlike my other friends, a little too cool for school. This didn't make his investment in our friendship seem strange; it was more like it wasn't fully accounted for. Still, he seemed sincere when he told me he liked the way I thought about things. *Look, ya gonna be a philosopher.* A philosopher? No kidding. I didn't even know it was a major you could study, let alone some kind of career option. But it sounded sophisticated and he had clearly succeeded in impressing me with myself. He was equally confident I would be a writer. *You gotta write. End of story.* A profession I at least knew existed but had seemed mostly speculative and out of reach until he uttered those words.

The point of all this is that he knew me pretty damn well. He knew my weaknesses (foremost among them that I could be a hypocrite, but that I hated being a hypocrite and was constantly fighting against it) and my strengths (foremost among them that I was almost as loyal as he was). Since loyalty had become a liability in my family, as will happen when you support opposing armies, I was grateful for a positive outlet for it.

This guy was the first of us to get real facial hair, the first to get his driver's license, the first fake ID, and the one with the best chance of buying beer without one. As I've already explained, it's not like you spent a lot of time back then trying to figure out who was gay because you didn't tend to believe anyone was, but in retrospect, he would have been literally the last person I would have expected to have any leanings in that direction.

The night in question, he was staying over at my dad's. Upstairs. I had the basement. I think we'd had a couple of beers out, then come back to watch *Saturday Night Live* or something like that and he'd gone up to bed. But then he reappeared twenty minutes later. I don't remember exactly what the setup was, but one minute he was standing there talking to me, and the next he'd pulled my underwear down far enough to get his mouth around me. And instead of calling him off right away, I not only continued to accept the favor, but returned it once the idea had been . . . suggested to me.

I'll have more to say about this later, but for the moment let me just point out the fact that another friendship was in the process of ending. With me increasingly ill at ease, and—before either of us had a chance to blow our load—telling him he should get back upstairs. After some unpleasant back and forth, he did go back upstairs, but it wasn't like that was going to fix everything (look at the super-straight guy putting in a boundary after he's spent the last few minutes with his head buried in his friend's crotch). No, here was what seemed like irrefutable proof I was gay—I'd gone from zero to hard in a microsecond—and it shook me to the core. Who the hell was I now? Not the same guy who always had a girlfriend. Not the same guy who'd spent the back half of his freshman year involved with an upperclasswoman he'd gotten pregnant. Until that night, most of my relationship existence had been wrapped around trying to deal with the fallout from that situation (short answer: not well). And now here was this. And I didn't deal well with this either.

It was a long—very long—ride up to school the next day. I drove along that highway telling myself I could have slept with a hundred more women in my life up until that point—a thousand—and it still wouldn't have canceled out what had just happened. And yet the more I thought about it, the more it didn't seem like this one experience should have canceled out all the women either. Trying to be the most absolutely honest with myself, I just didn't feel like I'd been faking it with the ladies. I did allow myself to consider my old boss's theory that it was like a lamp burning brighter, but I don't know, it seemed like all the lamps had been burning pretty bright, so I put that idea aside. I also tried thinking of it as a one-off before discarding that idea as well, realizing I was no longer in a position to be making predictions.

I told myself, look, your dick was obviously up for something like this and maybe it always had been. All the minor incidents and innuendo leading up to this point, and here was proof of *something*, even if I wasn't 100% sure what that something meant. I can't say I was happy about what had happened because I wasn't. In any way happy. But maybe there was a kind of backhanded relief, and, in any case, by the time I arrived back on campus, I was resigned to it.

Me: *You're probably wondering why I didn't bring this up sooner?*
Gay Inc.: *Not necessarily.*
Me: *Because you know if I thought I was a shoo-in for Gay Inc., I wouldn't have even bothered applying in the first place; I would just have taken a share in your company.*
Gay Inc.: *Of course. From what you've told me, you're not an automatic hire.*
Me: *What am I then?*
Gay Inc.: *Hm.* Pencil tapping. *I don't think I'm the one to answer that question. But I do know you still seem conflicted. We generally prefer our applicants to show a bit more enthusiasm for wanting to be here.*
Me: *Yeah. I don't blame you.*
Gay Inc.: *Undoubtedly, you've got some more reflecting to do. Don't think of this as a stopping point. Now that you've got this episode off your chest, why don't you take some time and look at the bigger picture. What happened next? What happened after that? See how it fits in with the rest of your life. And here.* Reaching across the desk. *Take my card and feel free to check back in. We're always here if you need us.*

What did happen next? Well, once I'd settled back in at college, I imagine I must have been testing myself on some level, wondering if I'd have any newfound urge to mess around with one of my fraternity brothers, waiting to see if I would have any physical interest in guys, period. But the longer I went without this happening, the more convinced I became that it wasn't likely to happen. I remained attracted to my friends for the same reason I'd been attracted to them in the first place. Because I enjoyed hanging out with them, not because I was interested in what their penises might look like. And when I met a new guy, the same criteria kept being applied.

Nothing changed with my relationships with women, either. I continued to go through girlfriends in much the way I had before. Intense beginnings, unhappy endings, and so it went. I'm sure there was some compartmentalization going on—and it wasn't like I would ever consider myself 100% straight again—but it was a lot of years after that of feeling fundamentally straight.

NEW ORLEANS

That didn't mean nothing of interest happened sexuality-wise during these years, although if someone had asked me about it when I first started going over this stuff, I wouldn't have thought I had much to offer. But the more I thought about it, the more I remembered, and before I knew it, I realized there was quite a bit of on-topic material to consider, and the question became, why had I forgotten?

These experiences didn't seem like the kinds of things I'd want to be hiding from myself, because they were overwhelmingly positive. And I think that probably has a lot do with the reason I'd originally overlooked them. Negative memories are far more likely to stick with you, and negative memories were what I had. Of being ambushed. By a former classmate, a former boss, a former best friend. But when it came time for me to go out and explore the world, I think I was better prepared to take whatever might happen in stride. Much less likely to be surprised by anything or anybody, least of all myself.

So there I was, armed with a philosophy degree and—in a development that's likely to shock no one—having a hard time figuring out what I wanted to do with my life. Sure, I wanted to write, but that wasn't the kind of thing you mentioned in polite company and besides, you still needed to work. Preferably as many unusual jobs in as many unusual places as possible so you could pay the rent and still have something interesting left over to fill the pages with.

Teaching assistant in Compton? Sounds good. *Pulling chain in a lumber mill in Idaho?* Can do. *Gas station attendant in the North Georgia mountains?* Why not? My first night in New Orleans I went to a corner store to see if it was possible to buy a beer after 2 a.m., and when the lady told me, "Honey, you can do anything you want, any time you want in this town," I guessed I'd be hanging around for a while.

I'd parked my grandmother's old Buick somewhere in the French Quarter, and after finishing that beer, went back and curled up in the back seat. I hadn't been asleep long, when I was awakened by some peculiar noises that sounded like they were coming from right beside my head—metal against metal. Trying to figure out what exactly the heck was going on, I rose up out of my sleeping bag barking HEY, and the guy who'd been trying to break into the car freaked. He yelled out like he'd seen a ghost and ran, dropping the crowbar he'd been using, which clattered onto the sidewalk.

I remember stepping out in my boxers, picking up the crowbar and smiling to myself. *Maybe this town's a little dangerous but I'm gonna make it fine here.* Still, I decided, if I was able to find a job, it would probably be wise to get an apartment sooner rather than later.

The place I ended up moving into turned out to be situated almost directly across from a gay bar. That bar pumped out disco music for what seemed like (and may actually have been) twenty-four hours a day, and while I remember occasionally wishing they'd give it a rest, that was likely the result of the frustration I was feeling that I couldn't always keep up with them.

I'd be coming back late from Snug Harbor, where they let waiters who'd just gotten off shift (or maybe anyone) in for free for the last set, or hosting an all-night poker game, or unable to sleep, trying to complete just one short story, and like the sun coming up in the morning, there was that four on the floor rhythm keeping endless time to everything.

I don't recall a desire either to stop by or to avoid the place—it was just there—but what I do think of as important was the distant sense of camaraderie I began to feel with the patrons. I'd never really had gay people in my life before and, even if we were mostly in each other's background, there was no doubt that we were all part of the same city.

There were at least a couple of guys I waited tables with who were gay. One of them—Max—brashly so. In the locker room, he'd regale us with stories of his exploits with minimal prompting. I dug how when the guys would ask him if he'd gotten any dick the previous night, it fit just as easily into the flow of conversation as when another guy got asked if he'd gotten any pussy. The pure democracy of it. And like pretty much everyone else I worked with at Arnaud's—from the former prize fighter who told me the best way to toughen myself up was to shadowbox and lift imaginary weights, to the easygoing when sober, dark when drunk gambler whose tag line was "Came to New Orleans for a Funeral and Never Left"—Max was just one more character in the mix.

The only time I really questioned him was the night he recounted the story of a party he'd recently been to. One of the guests had passed out on the floor with his belt unbuckled, his pants maybe partway down (Max was a little sketchy on the details here) and, apparently, everyone at the party had proceeded to take a turn with him. Needless to say, this was a far more serious consequence for passing out than had occurred at my fraternity (where you were liable to have a single eyebrow shaved off), and I remember thinking, *Isn't that rape*? Most of the guys in the locker room had just shaken their heads like it wasn't the most dramatic thing they'd heard that day, but one of the older waiters had been openly disgusted about it.

Max was quick to cut him off. His smile becoming a smirk, his obvious relish in telling the story turning to indignation. "What did he expect was going to happen, his pants weren't even all the way on? I'd bet half my tips that boy'd been fantasizing about getting banged the entire night." I picked up the other side of the argument from there, saying something along the lines of even if it was a fantasy, couldn't there be some daylight between that and what he wanted to happen in reality? And how could Max possibly know what the guy really wanted since he'd never bothered to ask? But he just tsk tsked me, saying actions spoke louder than words. The takeaway for me here was there was a subset of gay men who were pretty indistinguishable from their straight counterparts when it came to embracing the idea of "asking for it."

New Orleans was the first place I ever went to a movie theater by myself, and I liked the experience so much it became a regular feature of my life there, and then, afterward, a lifelong habit. One of the films I saw during this time was *My Own Private Idaho*. I'd been intrigued with River Phoenix since high school, when my friends and I had gone to see *Stand by Me* and, like most everyone else, been blown away by both the movie and his performance in it. Also, like probably every other group of friends who went to see it, we had a field day pointing out the similarities between us and the main characters. Phoenix and I were just about the same age, and I'm as guilty as the next moviegoer in believing I had some kind of connection with him, feeling like he had information that I needed to better understand.

I believed this and yet I have to admit to being torn about going to see *Idaho*. I knew there'd be gay content, and was I seriously not going to see it because of that? The fact that I'd had any debate at all showed I still wasn't comfortable in my own skin, but fortunately, Phoenix settled the matter for me himself when asked whether his fans would be upset that he was playing gay. His response: "Fuck 'em." Or, more likely (because it was a magazine interview and no one much printed profanities back then), "F— 'em." Either way, I was like, good point.

Going into the matinee, I felt like a newly initiated member of some mildly seedy club. Noting the dozen or so middle-aged guys spread out almost perfectly spaced apart among the seats, I felt both relieved (thinking this would mean no shenanigans on the side), and also a kind of nostalgia for the future. *Watch,* I said to myself, *this will be you in twenty years.* Thinking that probably wouldn't be the end of the world, I chose a similarly sequestered seat, and by the time my eyes had adjusted to the darkened theater I'd made my peace with the whole situation.

I thoroughly enjoyed the movie. And while I didn't pop a boner, I did know I had no problem with anything that'd happened on screen.[4] There'd been an achingly sad scene by a campfire—one which Phoenix wrote himself—where one guy tries to reach out more intimately to another and doesn't quite get there. And the hustling both these guys did on the side struck me as a legitimate way to get by no matter what your orientation. Phoenix had made the job seem almost romantic, and there was no getting around the fact that he hadn't just been convincing as a hustler, but—even though I wouldn't have used the word at the time because I didn't have full access to it—sexy.

I couldn't find Phoenix's "fuck 'em" quote when I tried to research it online, but I did find an impression about the actor from *Out* magazine.[5] The writer, James Bagget, describes an

---

[4] There are exactly three films that've given me a full-on erection while watching in a theater: *Bound* (lesbian scene), *A History of Violence* (heterosexual scene) and, yes, *Brokeback Mountain* (two straight actors in a tent). Textbook examples of my sexuality that I should hesitate to mention only because they're a little too neat and tidy, but the main reason I'm reluctant to do so is because I realize the theme among them is not pure sex, but sex cut to varying degrees with violence, and even if it was between couples of a kind, I'm not fully at ease with the implications.

[5] http://www.angelfire.com/film/riverphoenix/out.html

evening he spent with River and his girlfriend, and while he's careful not to peg him as anything sexuality-wise, he does make note of a long series of questions River asks him about being gay, starting with, "When did you first know you were gay?" Mr. Baggett's conclusion: "He was asking me these questions because he could . . .without being pegged a queer. I was safe. I was obviously gay. And we were with his girlfriend."

Now there's a history of gay men using women, usually with their knowledge, as beards—public companions to give the illusion of straightness—and, to his credit, Mr. Baggett goes through great pains to show that's not what's happening here. There's not a shred of solid evidence to suggest Phoenix was gay. And yet, if I'm interpreting it correctly, Phoenix shows not just a curiosity toward gay life—but a comfort with that curiosity—that was probably a half step ahead of mine at the time, but still on the same path in terms of an increasing openness to it.

If you read interviews with Phoenix's girlfriend at the time, you're struck by how much his memory sticks with her all these years later, and without pretending to have any idea what went on between them, you feel like their relationship was the real deal. I mention this because when I was living in New Orleans, I was in the throes of some pretty intense feelings toward someone, myself, and rather than making me feel conflicted about alternative lifestyles, it helped me be confident enough to look around and mostly appreciate what else was going on out there.

When I say, "intense feelings" toward someone, what I mean to say is, "a little obsessed." Over the years, watching friends fall into this kind of pattern, I'd always felt slightly superior, thinking, *That's never gonna happen to me.* But then it did.

(You can only hope if you find yourself in this situation that it happens when you're younger, because obsession turns out by definition to be a distraction from everything else you're trying to accomplish in your life, but goes along quite well when your biggest responsibility is crumbing someone's dinner table.)

How obsessed was I? Well, when I was boxing at the New Orleans Athletic Club, I held my own pretty well, but this one cop used to just kick the shit out of me every time we sparred, and one day after I'd left the ring with him, showered up, and was walking back to my place, I noticed something funky was happening with my eye. The woman I was a little obsessed with was flying in to visit that weekend, and my first thought was, *I can't be dealing with this right now.* As the day wore on, the problem was getting harder and harder to ignore, and by the time I picked her up at the airport, I was half-blind in my right eye. Thinking there was no way she'd flown in just to hang out at the hospital (we had plans for, among other things, JazzFest), I never said a word to her about it the whole debaucherous weekend.

Stoicism's a funny thing. It's hard to tell in the moment if you're being admirably tough or unaccountably stupid, but you usually figure it out sooner or later. For me, what solved it wasn't checking into Charity Hospital on the way back from the airport, the young surgeon shaking his head at me and telling me how close I was to losing my sight. It wasn't what happened a few weeks later, me peeling back the bandages and wondering what, if anything, I'd be able to see. What did do it was getting chewed out by the woman a couple months later when I finally told her what had happened. She was furious, telling me how fucked up I'd been, how I wasn't a hero, how I'd put her in a shitty position by never giving her the chance to insist I get it looked at. And by the time she'd calmed down enough to tell me she was sorry it'd happened, I was more than clear on the fact that my decision had fallen into the unaccountably stupid category.

What can I say? I wasn't the only guy who felt this way about her, and like the competition, even though I was technically between girlfriends, I could almost pretend she was mine from time to time. She is the one and only person in my life who ever gave me a stiffy just listening to her voice on the phone and it didn't matter at all what we were talking about. (She was also the first woman I ever got nervous messing around with when we were actually together, which almost made sense.) She would get all quiet, not quite sweet, say some random thing and it was like this direct connection to something inside me. I never did figure out what.

The point of all this is to underline how far away I was from worrying about my sexuality during this time. What I was worried about was my sanity. *How could I be so interested in someone who seemed to bring out my most unhealthy behaviors?* And yet, feeling so far gone in my attraction for her, I imagine it was easier for me to brush up against a variety of queer happenings, absorb them to some degree, and keep whistling down the road.

Whether I was in possession of a car or not, I preferred hitchhiking to any other mode of travel in my twenties, and wanting to impress the woman with this fact, I'd made a point of thumbing my way into Texas to spend time with her. It had been a quiet day, and I was walking along a stretch of frontage road, when I spotted an old pickup come puttering down the road toward me. As it was coming from the opposite direction, it was easy to keep track of its turtle-like progress, and I was reminded of that scene in *The Holy Grail* where the knight is storming the castle, drum roll in the background, except they keep cutting the drum roll and restarting it, sending the guy back to the copse of trees he'd originally emerged from and making it appear like he really isn't getting anywhere. Then, suddenly, he's at the gate.

I believe the truck window was already rolled down when the guy stuck his head out of it. "Do you like men, son?"

Not even a hello, mind you, but I smiled at him anyway, an easy response coming to my lips. "I don't believe I'll need a ride, sir, thank you." And then him nodding and puttering off again down the road.

I can't tell you what a relief it was not to be getting my panties in a wad just because someone had propositioned me. It felt like a breakthrough of sorts, not to be on the defensive, and I realized how much I'd managed to chill out on the subject. When I first started working at Arnaud's, Max or one of his allies had noticed I was reading a copy of Nietzsche's *The Gay Science* and had been all tittery about it. I tried to explain it was a philosophy book, but it felt like I was wasting my breath and sure enough, I was henceforth on the receiving end of a number of tame—but flirty—comments. I hadn't been thrilled about them in the beginning, but over the course of my time there, in the restaurant and around the city, I'd come to realize how nice it was to have any human being feel like you were worth the flirt. So when the pale-blue pickup rolled up that day, I was ready for it. (Granted, it was slim pickings on an otherwise deserted road, so his proposal didn't qualify as compliment of the year or anything, but still.)[6]

SANTA FE

New Orleans was getting too hot to think about staying there through the summer, so after my six-month lease had ended, I bounced around with a couple odd jobs in the Southeast before finding myself living out of my grandmother's car again. Working my way toward California, because isn't that where people tend to go when they feel lost? I'd gotten as far as Santa Fe and had set up shop temporarily on the St. John's campus, where they had an incredibly large bathroom off the library. You could shut *and lock* the door and really soap yourself off, shave, start your morning like a regular person.

I was exploring the town during the day and then bedding down in the back seat at the end of it, which went fine until one night when I awoke to a loud banging on the window. Some headway had apparently been made since the break-in attempt in New Orleans as this person wasn't trying to be underhanded about it, but I was still a little rattled and it took me a while to find my key to put in the ignition to get the electric window down. The delay meant even more banging, but finally I was able to open the window a bit and there was Campus Security shining a beam in my face and wanting to know if I went to school there. "Not exactly," I told her. (I'd attended one of Charles Bell's evening philosophy lectures that week, did that count?) She then managed to look even more ornery. "Then

[6] For all the hitchhiking I did, this was the one and only time a guy made an obvious move to pick me up. And it was always guys in America. Women gave me rides in other countries but never here in the States.

you're going to have to leave or I'm calling the police."

Now, not only was this in the middle of the night, in the middle of a bitterly cold February, but it was also in the middle of a snowstorm and I was having a hard time accepting the fact that she was really standing there hassling me. I thought, *Shouldn't you be in your little patrol car with the heater on and eating a donut or something,* really put out about it, the way only a young person can be when they feel like the whole world owes them something. I tried blowing her off.

"I'll be gone in the morning," I told her. But she wasn't having any of it.

So I drove down toward Albuquerque half-dressed and bleary-eyed, the car slipping and sliding until the elevation dropped going down La Bajada hill, the ice melting along with it. But as I approached the I-40 interchange to head further west, I realized I wasn't going to take the exit, and pulled over a short time later. Those clever folks who altered New Mexico's slogan from Land of Enchantment to Land of Entrapment probably had me in mind as I considered my options. For whatever reason, Santa Fe was calling me back, and I had a job and a place to live there less than twenty-four hours later.

My housing arrangements were ideal for a while. I was paying half-rent on a place I had almost exclusively to myself, with my forty-something roommate staying with his girlfriend up on Canyon Road. But when she broke up with him after about six weeks, he returned home and started spiraling almost immediately. He'd wake me up in the middle of the night, drunk, volume blasting on the stereo, telling me on pretty much every occasion that he was certain I was his long-lost brother from Czechoslovakia. Then he would bare his sorrows, the outpourings usually bookended by him hugging me.

Even though my friends and I hug now, we never did back then, and this took some getting used to. Clearly, the reality of guy-hugs was failing to live up to the dream. If anything, I was reminded of the times I'd tried to console my mom and sister in the period after my dad left, and going with this theme tried to act like he was, indeed, family. Putting my arms around him and offering whatever genius advice I had available for someone with twice the life experience. It wasn't the hugging that did me in—my hugging career kind of took off from there, now that I think of it. It was reaching some sort of threshold on the amount of depressing material I could take in. Even though I liked the guy, I knew I wasn't going to be long for that house.

Fast forward another month or so, and I was living in a little blue Walmart tent in the forest above Santa Fe. Feeling literally rich, with bartending tips stuffed into my pockets, and no housing expenses or bills of any kind to pick at them. Before long, my new girlfriend and our wolf pup had moved into the tent with me, and not long after that, two more people from work had moved up into the forest, one guy only about twenty minutes down the trail from us. Our girlfriends were friends, and with the ladies taking the day shifts and the guys the nights, I hung out with him a fair bit.

Vince was a great guy and an amazing poet. I'd been trying to take my writing seriously since New Orleans—meaning, I was actually trying to write rather than just daydreaming about it—but was still filled with doubts about the wisdom of the entire enterprise. And along comes this guy who makes this seem not only like a legitimate—but an essential—way to spend time. Listening to his polished pieces I realized I had a ways to go, but I figured he was a couple of years older and there was time to catch up.

He introduced me to the poetry of Galway Kinnell (who I could handle) and the prose of Cormac McCarthy (who intimidated me too much, although his description of a boy tracking a wolf in *The Crossing* would become my single go-to example of flawless storytelling). At the time, my buddy was pushing *The Orchard Keeper*, reading his favorite lines out loud like incantations. He'd be like, "Close your eyes and listen to this shit." He also handed me a copy of Denis Johnson's *Jesus Son* (the bar we worked at also had a bookstore in the front, another insanely good setup). *Jesus Son* was, of course, perfect. I was a sucker for any gritty story line at that age, but the upshot of the book had little to do with the grittiness.

The narrator—who's already recounted a previous entanglement with a woman—is riding the El in Chicago and at one of the stops he decides to follow another guy off. He trails him to a laundromat, where the guy recognizes him from the train. "You were on the El," the guy says, and the narrator turns away, trying to hide an erection. "I knew men got that way about men," he says, "but I didn't know I did." I couldn't believe it was there on the page. I reread it like a half-dozen times thinking, *Hey, maybe I'm not the only fucknut out there with mixed feelings about sexuality. Maybe it's all more complicated than people are letting on.* You have to remember, this was before the internet was running at full throttle, and chat rooms and message boards for each and every proclivity were still getting built out. When it was easy to salivate over any breadcrumb you were tossed. It was the one of the best gifts of my twenty-third year—this instant one-verse Bible—and I held it close to the chest.

And right along with *Jesus Son* came my buddy's own poetry to make it even more interesting. I can't remember whether he showed me the book first or read me this one particular poem, but it didn't matter, they dovetailed together. Because this one poem was about two guys messing around in a dumpster and it contained the line, "Your turn to be the girl, now."

Now, by this point in my life, I was clear on the fact that somewhere in the United States, maybe even outside that very bar at that very moment, two guys could well be fucking around in a dumpster. And one of those guys could've been me. And one of those guys could've been the guy standing in front of me reading his poetry. It's not like I have any idea what he actually got up to in the bedroom (or on the floor of his tent), but if he hadn't messed around with another guy before, he obviously didn't seem to have a major problem with the concept. And knowing how tight he and his girlfriend seemed to be, this meant I was having an encounter with another living, breathing human being who was quite possibly neither gay nor straight.

It was a good poem. When he got to that line, my heart barely skipped a beat. My face didn't turn red and I didn't look away. If anything, I was drawn to the edginess of it, and when I walked away afterward, my respect for the guy, and for myself, went directly up.

I think I was able to put that relationship in such a positive light because of what didn't happen. Meaning, he didn't make a move on me. It's one thing to have a stranger roll down their window and try to pick you up on the highway, but it would've been another to have yet another friend try to pull off the same thing, and I just know I wouldn't have had the same reaction if I'd been convinced he wanted to get in my pants.

At this point, I can scan back over my early life and feel pretty confident about the times when a guy was actually trying to pick me up, when I didn't snap to it or wasn't prepared to snap to it, but this didn't seem like one of those times. I mean, this is the guy who would sometimes drop by the campsite in the morning and—whether I was reading under a tree or sprawled out, clothesless, on the rocks—his approach with me was always the same. *Hey, dude, what's up?* and then we'd start talking about whatever fiction or philosophy book I'd put down beside me.

Looking back, I'm all but certain this experience would have sent me back a few squares if this guy reading me his poem or giving me that book had just been pretexts for a hookup. How it would only have taken me longer to get to the respectable place I was heading toward and did, eventually, arrive at. It wasn't only that I wouldn't have been into any physical contact at the time. I wouldn't have been into having a big discussion about it, either, and I think he wisely sensed this. Our conversations were always literary, never personal. Which made them easier to share with my girlfriend—in a genuinely casual way—because that was the way the guy had taught me they should be presented.

THE FIREFIGHTER, THE WOMAN, AND THE WOLF

I tried and tried to avoid this next section. You should've seen all the cheap little segues I originally attempted to get me from Santa Fe to San Francisco without having to delve into any of the messier material in between. But, inevitably, someone will want to know what happened, and as I'm trying not to be a coward about this stuff, I'm gonna go ahead and give you my best shot at an explanation. For everyone else, meaning those who don't want to get bogged down in the details, consider this a reader's advisory, whereby you're being advised to skip it. There's next to nothing about sex in here, it gets a little depressing at points, and in general you'd have to do a little more work to understand why it fits in with the topic of sexuality.

Over the next several years, I managed to get pretty darn close to being an adult. I felt like I was becoming someone—not like I'd been a poser in high school or college, but I would've been hard pressed to define myself very well back then. *So this was what it felt like to have an identity?* The repetition of certain behaviors and feelings and thoughts creating strands inside you that begin to pull solid. I was in love—with my job, my woman, and the wolf pup we were raising together. And when I turned my back on all of them, I should've realized what I was really turning my back on was the self I'd been in the process of creating.

THE FIREFIGHTER

Before I made a bunch of questionable decisions, I made one really good one, and that was to turn down a scholarship to get my PhD in Philosophy in favor of joining the local fire department. It felt inevitable, in a way. When I'd been boxing in New Orleans, in addition to that ass-kicking cop I regularly sparred with, there'd been a group of firefighters who were often at the gym at the same time as I was. Their captain was the one who'd spent the most time training me, and one day, with the two of us still catching our breath from jumping rope, he said, "Listen, me and the guys have been talking and we think you'd fit in over at the station. You ever give any thought to becoming a firefighter?" It was just a flash when he'd said it—*Yeah, I think that might really happen*—and then it was gone, and I was left awkwardly thanking him for the idea, hemming and hawing about this and that, since I had no idea what I wanted to be doing.

His question hung with me, though.

I wasn't a particularly respectful kid, but I respected this guy a lot, and for all the twists and turns my life took after that day at the gym, you could just about make out the straight line that led from his suggestion to my putting my signature on the paperwork in Santa Fe. Convinced by then that I was meant for the job.

I can't say my dad shared my enthusiasm. He'd spent the summer warming to the idea that I'd finally be staying in one place—getting my degree, with no tuition expense and being paid a generous monthly stipend. When I broke the news of the plan change, we were on the phone, and even though I never once saw him drunk, or buzzed (or even with a drink in his hand unless he was chanting something in Hebrew), he kept a running tally of his drinks that night. My dad's sister and brother-in-law were into wine, his wife had recently gotten into wine, and my dad was giving a glass a try at the end of the day to help him unwind. But he told me he'd already had the one and announced he was gonna pour himself another. There was a pause while he took an audible gulp . . .and then he just let loose. A complete and total mockery of my decision, and the more he drank, the more sarcastic he got. Mostly, I let him have the floor, figuring there were bound to be other dads out there who would've had a similar reaction. Plus, my father just wasn't a sarcastic man, and even though I was feeling defensive, I was more in awe of the roll he was on. I can't remember the entire speech, but one part stands out. "So you're gonna run around with a hose and put out fires, is that it? A fire hose? You think you have a big enough hose to handle it?"

So totally unlike him, but I mention it only because, well, I just love this story about my dad. I know he only wanted the best for me and was just struggling to figure me out. And besides, it wasn't like he washed his hands of the whole situation. After I'd graduated from the academy, he sent me a letter giving his tacit approval by congratulating me while also letting me know he'd done some research. "EVIDENTLY, THE TWO MAIN PROBLEMS [WITH FIREFIGHTERS] SEEM TO BE DRINKING AND GAMBLING, IN THAT ORDER." (Dad typed in ALL CAPS.) And after he'd returned home from a visit to New Mexico, I was told by multiple sources that he'd taken to wearing the SFFD cap I'd given him pretty much everywhere he went outside the office. Proudly, yes, but I imagine even more than that, because he'd seen how happy I was.

That firefighters regularly top the charts in terms of job satisfaction doesn't surprise me in the least.[7] I never could've imagined being okay with the alarm going off in the morning and heading into work, but most days I was. Once I got my butt in gear, I even started going in early, to relieve other guys at the end of their "twenty-fours," because that's what you wanted done for you. It's not that firefighters never bitch and moan about their job. There's going to be complaints about pay, and time

[7] https://www.bloomberg.com/news/articles/2019-07-17/which-jobs-make-people-the-happiest-in-america?srnd=premium https://superscholar.org/features/the-10-happiest-and-10-unhappiest-professions/

off, and being held over, and who's being promoted and who's not. You're going to see some awful stuff and you're going to have your bad days. What made it different, for me at least, was not simply having great days to balance out the bad ones. It was that almost all the rest of the days in between were good, not mediocre. While I was at the department, there was only one guy who took more overtime than I did (and he was saving up to buy a Harley), and I would've taken even more if it was the only job I was working.

I don't want to spoil it by saying too much. Yeah, being part of a crew's like being part of a family, dysfunctions and all. Yeah, most firefighters are, in fact, good people. You can go to pretty much any firehouse in the country—which we always did when we traveled anywhere to trade T-shirts—and meet similar types of guys and gals who you'd be happy to have as neighbors. But the thing—the priceless thing—that the job has built into it that many other jobs don't, is that you never question if what you're doing is worthwhile.

When our younger boy's friend recently made some noise about wanting to become a firefighter, I couldn't have been more supportive of the idea. Same goes for the kid who Uber-ed me back home from the car repair shop and was thinking about joining up. It's easier now to hear the sirens when I'm in town, knowing most of my buddies have retired, and that, finally, I'm too old for it. But after I resigned, the regret never quite went away, and I had to use all my powers of persuasion to tell myself I was making the right choice.

I made it till just shy of my twenty-seventh birthday. My stated reason for leaving was that we didn't have enough fires, and we didn't. So when I put in my notice, it was with the full intention of shifting over to wildland firefighting that summer. But the precipitating cause for my leaving was a personnel change at my station— a pretty adolescent reason for thinking about a career change and typical impulsive crap from me at that age—and if I'd only stayed with the department a while longer, they ended up creating a wildland firefighting unit. One I surely would have joined, and then maybe I could've had the best of both worlds. But it wasn't to be. As my dad wondered about in the same letter, "THE REAL QUESTION IS WHETHER YOU WILL STAY WITH IT."

THE WOMAN

You'll soon notice this section is the shortest of the three, and you're welcome to have your way with that fact, but to cut to the chase, I'll tell you that the night of our first date, I called up my sister and told her this was the woman I was going to marry. And sure enough, it wasn't long before she'd moved into the tent with me, and then the tent became a house, with all the joys of waking up in the same bed countered with the bill managing and Christmas card sending that went along with it. Overall, things felt like they were falling into place, but I'll defer again to my dad here, who'd already seen the writing on the wall.

"YOU KNOW IN MY OPINION YOU'VE GOT THE ABSOLUTE BEST THERE BUT NEEDLESS TO SAY WHETHER YOU CAN WEATHER LIFE'S PROBLEMS IS GOING TO BE UP TO THE TWO OF YOU. ONE THING IS FOR CERTAIN, THOUGH, IF YOU BOTH DON'T HAVE A TOTALLY OPEN LINE OF COMMUNICATION IT ISN'T GOING TO HAPPEN. IN THIS REGARD I CERTAINLY

WORRY MORE ABOUT YOU THAN I DO HER, SINCE YOU SEEM TO HAVE ONE OF THE NEGATIVE [my mom's side of the family] CHARACTERISTICS, WHICH IS TO KEEP TOO MUCH INSIDE ONESELF." *What the hell was he talking about?* I prided myself on keeping things inside. Emotional talks just wrung it out of you to seemingly no great purpose. *How could this be a negative?*

Underlining the point, I shoved down any nascent concerns I had about the letter right along with the very kinds of relationship feelings he'd been referring to in it. Feelings like, "I don't know if I'm ready to have a mortgage," and "Suppose I don't want to consult with anyone else about decisions that I make." I was still under the impression that being 110% behind something—100% of the time—was a realistic goal. So if I was going to do something properly, I couldn't have truck with any doubts.

This kind of strategy would work a lot better if when you banished worries and negative feelings, they went away—far away—and stayed there. But they don't. The little buggers go somewhere inside you where they can lie dormant for long periods—so long that you forget they're even in there—but then something happens one day, you let down your guard, and you realize not only have they stuck around, but they've been quietly building themselves into a formidable army, and suddenly they're the ones in charge. Your 110% certainty that things are going to work becomes 110% certainty that they won't.

It's even worse than it sounds because not only have you built up a false confidence in yourself, you're so convincing you've simultaneously managed to build up real confidence in those around you. In your partner, your partner's family, your family. They've had even less warning about what's coming than you, and it can be pretty shattering when you announce it's all over.

I knew I was getting close to the end of the line with this whole business, because while explaining to yet another partner why things weren't going to work out between us, this time I cried. Something I hadn't done in years. My stated reason for losing faith in the relationship was that we were better lovers than friends, and I wanted someone I could have a conversation with. Twelve thousand conversations with hundreds of other people later, I can safely say my reasoning didn't stand the test of time.

THE WOLF

Wolf hybrids are pretty common in New Mexico. They need lots of space, and that's just what the state is composed of, so it's a good place to raise one. When a co-worker mentioned her family's she-wolf was about to have a litter, both my woman's and my ears perked up. If it had just been me thinking about getting one, that would have been one thing, but seeing as my woman was so consistently responsible, I figured she knew what we'd be getting ourselves into. Sure, our living situation in the forest was going to be difficult to manage with her returning to acupuncture school in fall, and, yes, it would have only taken one good winter storm to overwhelm our little tent. But it was summer. The pups were irresistible. And so we picked out our favorite while he was still living in the den, came back for him when he was ready to venture out in the world, and named him Aquila. After the leader of the pack in *The Jungle Books*—I'd been reading the stories aloud by firelight—but also after the constellation. Its brightest star being one of three that compose the Summer Triangle, the guide to pretty much everything in the night sky, which I learned, by heart, that summer.

I've had the pleasure of caring for three dogs in my life whose personalities roughly coincided with my personality when I had them: wild in my twenties, semi-wild in my thirties, and a little bit of wild left over to go along with my forties. Aquila was the wild one. And I mean wild in the most beautiful sense of the word. His spirit so far surpassed anything domesticated—canine or human—that you would have needed your vision checked if you mistook him for a dog. His mother was true wolf, ninety percent, wicked clever with otherworldly yellow eyes. She moved like a ghost, and barely let anyone handle her. His father was a wolf-Shepherd mix, a high energy but sweet-natured giant. Aquila took the best from both of them.

It's hard to pick just one thing that stood out about him, but I'll go with affectionate. Certainly, more so than I was at the time we got him. He'd never hesitate to jump up on the bed after (or occasionally during) sex, trying to lick both of us, my woman giggling, and me shaking my head as I picked him up and deposited him back on the floor. But he always wormed his way back in with us sooner or later.

He could also be fiercely independent. Obeying ninety-five percent of the time meant he generally agreed to go along with what you wanted and otherwise threw you a bone or two along the way, but if he got it in his head he wanted to chase an elk for miles then that's what he was going to do, and we knew we never really owned him.

I'm only aware of him barking two times in his life. Once,

at some random guy passing on the trail leading up to our campsite; I had a bad feeling about the guy, too, but I'll never fully understand what that was about. The second time Aquila went absolutely nuts on this other guy who I didn't know well, but I was friendly with his wife, and found out later from a mutual friend that he was beating her. As a plan was being worked on to try to help get her out of the situation, I remember looking at Aquila and thinking, *Who's educating who about the world around here?*

Raising an animal is a long way from raising a child, but then again, it's not nothing. I took to telling friends, "You really should get a pet first before thinking about having kids and see how you do." I knew I'd made my share of immature decisions with Aquila, and it was on the basis of those decisions that I felt sure I wasn't ready to start a family.

It seemed like we were on the path to that, though. Loving him, feeding him, teaching him, learning from him, protecting him, watching him grow. He used to curl up around my shoulders while I was driving, two paws on one side of my head, two on the other, and at a certain point I was like, *Man, you've gotta be fifty pounds by now* (on the way to one hundred thirty), *you can't do this anymore.* But I let him get away with it beyond what was practically sensible. Just like I let him get away with jumping up on me when I'd walk in the door at the end of my shift, him having convinced himself he could operate just as well on two legs, trying to wrestle me down. Unfortunately, he then felt this was an appropriate greeting for anyone who happened to walk in the house, and once he'd taken down the first grandma, I realized this maybe hadn't been the best idea (both grandmas learned to brace themselves against the nearest wall immediately upon entry).

Aquila was a presence. And the one constant in my life. I ended up with primary custody after his mother and I split, and he was living with me and a college girlfriend I'd become re-involved with when I put in my notice at the department. We had a little gap of time before I would report to the Forest Service and Skelly would start graduate classes at UNM in Albuquerque, so we decided to spend it on a piece of land I'd put some money down on the previous year. The land was surrounded by forest with a little stream running through it, fifty-nine miles from my station, because fire department regulations were you had to live within sixty. I'd hoped to be able to save up enough to build on it one day; ideally, before retirement. Now, having just left my job, I was more than a little worried about the payments long term, but didn't see why we shouldn't enjoy it in the meantime. Aquila seemed totally in his element there—with water being so scarce in New Mexico, he couldn't get enough of that stream—and we arrived with the tipi we'd put up the previous fall waiting for us.

Our first priority was to put up a coyote fence around the tipi so we could let Aquila out in the morning or at night without worrying about him wandering. We cut and gathered the posts and were a little more than a third of the way through the job the morning I rolled up the door flap to let him out. I'd planned on following right along after him, but instead, curled up in bed for a few more minutes of warmth and fell back to sleep. When I got up again, he was gone.

We called, searched, called again. Got in the truck and drove down the dirt road, finally running into someone who said they'd just seen him. Aquila was an escape artist. He'd once hurdled over a six-foot wall to break out of an outdoor kennel when we'd gone away on a trip. Granted, I was standing on the other side of it, about to pick him up, but he could get out of most places if he really wanted to. I knew this, I knew he went exploring from time to time, but that morning I'd made it easy for him. I always had a bit of a bad feeling when I called and he didn't come right away, but no bad feeling could have prepared me for what came next.

Aquila had gotten in with some sheep and the rancher who owned them had just shot him. His body was still warm when I reached it. This might sound unnecessarily harsh if you live in a city, but this is oftentimes the way it goes out West, people are trying to make a living, and even in the moment, I understood the dynamics of the situation. I only had one question for the rancher. I believe he still had the gun in his hand when I walked up to him, looked him in the eye, and asked it. "Why didn't you give me a chance to make it up to you? Why? I would've paid you *anything*." Aquila had a collar and was known back in that valley, but it's not like the guy had any obvious reason to be ashamed until I tried to give him one. I feel like there was a flicker of guilt in his eyes when he briefly imagined how it could've turned out different, but maybe it was just a reflection of my own. In any case, he didn't have an answer, offering, instead, to help carry the body back to the truck. But I just shook my head. I couldn't speak any more.

Recently, I checked in with Skelly about what happened that day. I didn't remember breaking down or sobbing and she confirmed that. What she did remember was the same compulsive behavior I did—the constant need to reach up to my face with the back of my hand to wipe off whatever was there. Tears, it turned out, but I didn't fully recognize them at the time. It was a strange way to cry. Little awareness of it, no sounds, just a constant weeping, water leaking out of my eyes, blood staining everything, everywhere, as I picked up Aquila's stiffening body and carried him to the truck, where we loaded him in and drove away.

Naturally, I blamed myself. I kept picturing me all nestled in bed, dreaming some stupid dream, my back to the world no matter which way I was facing, while Aquila began his last adventure. I couldn't talk about it with anyone for a long time, but you can be sure I had plenty to say to myself. *What were you thinking going back to sleep? You would've had that fence done in two days, why didn't you keep a closer eye on him until then? You couldn't even take care of a creature who could mostly take care of himself.* And all those comments I'd had over the years about what a great dad I'd make, all the times I'd half gone in on them myself, even knowing I wasn't ready yet, vanished. Of course, I wasn't going to have a family, a normal job, a normal life. I wasn't responsible enough. And I wasn't sure I ever would be.

And now there was no chance of trying to put the pieces back together again. You see, I could've gotten rehired at the fire department. Chief told me on my last day that as long as he remained in charge, the job was mine if I ever wanted it back. It'd only been weeks and I was already missing it. And the woman who'd applauded loudest when I graduated from the academy? The acupuncturist who'd pushed me to grow up—too hard at times, if only I'd been able to find the words to tell her that—her love was made of the strongest stuff, and she, too, would almost certainly have taken me back if I'd gotten down on my knees and stayed there long enough. But the wolf we'd raised was gone forever.

The woman drove out to the land that day to say goodbye to Aquila. I'd spent the rest of the morning digging his grave, and as we held hands and stared down into it, there was nothing to do but silently mourn what had been lost.

BETWEEN

An object in motion tends to remain in motion and, sure enough, I continued to coast along, telling myself how hard it would have been for Aquila to stay in Albuquerque while I was off fighting fires. It was a small consolation. I missed him. All of him but especially his rough and tumble energy that, combined with my own, had made the household feel like it was complete. Fortunately, I didn't have to wait long for fire season to start, but when the Forest Service job I'd been all but guaranteed fell through at the last minute, I could feel things grinding to a halt. I waitlisted with other crews, but checking the messages at the end of each day to see if one of them had called me up, I couldn't help but wonder if the universe was trying to tell me something.

I can't pinpoint the exact moment when the polarity switched—when the New Mexico I'd once been so drawn toward started feeling like it was pushing me to leave—but practically everything there was a reminder of one careless decision or another and I'd grown weary of replaying them in my head. So I'd started to replay other ideas. About how maybe I wasn't who I thought I was. About how I was almost twenty-seven years old—an adult, or close to one by most any standard—and had better figure myself out soon. I'd become increasingly preoccupied with my failed relationships, and then, by extension, my sexuality, but having gone through everything in my head without coming to any definite conclusions, I felt like I was hitting a wall. Meanwhile, I was getting restless waiting to hear back from the Forest Service, and as I weighed the idea that maybe I should just get out of town—at least, for a little while—I reminded myself there were only two people worth sticking around for anyway. And further, that if they'd been the type to pressure me to stay, they wouldn't have been those people.

Ren was the guy I'd hit it off with first day at Fire Academy. A steady soldier returned from Iraq who enabled me to put into regular practice everything I'd learned about a certain kind of male friendship. Actions over words. Determining the favor the other guy needed so he didn't have to ask for it. Then being there when you said you would be. Every time. It was one of those relationships where both people give fifty-one percent, so you know the math is gonna work out, and I'd come to understand that those were the only kind worth taking seriously.

Of course, we mostly just had a blast together—rock climbing in Diablo Canyon, waterskiing on Abiquiu Lake, road trips on the bikes—but it's easy to have fun with pretty much anyone in your twenties and not have it mean a lot without a foundation of respect.

I remember when the fire department was giving a presentation on all the special housing programs available for married firefighters and, without batting an eyelash, Ren asked if he and I were to get a place together, would we be entitled to the same benefits. While the speaker guffawed his way through a "Probably not" (which only made the rest of the cadets in the room laugh harder), Ren waited. Then he pushed for an explanation. He didn't like the injustice of it, as he didn't like it anywhere he found it, one of the many things I admired him for

It wasn't a question of physical attraction between us, though I liked looking at him, or romantic attraction, though we shared some intimate moments. I was going to say it was pure attraction, but maybe that's a cheat, not saying anything at all. If there's such a thing as an attraction where you know you will be loyal to someone, richer or poorer, in sickness and in health—with no ring required—then that would be it.

An attraction like that can be expressed in many ways, but we chose to put all our feeling into the handshake we greeted each other and then signed off with. It wasn't too fancy, with a resounding clap that both echoed all the ones that'd come before it, and reaffirmed everything between us, fresh.

Skelly and I didn't have a cool handshake, but it was a similar kind of attraction expressed differently. Our first kiss was one of two I remembered well in my life (Coles Tower, 15th floor, on a clear day you could see the ocean from up there), and even with college receding further into the rearview, she was still having an impact. Skelly's approval meant something to me in a way that other people's didn't, and I invariably found myself admiring her thoughts, her words, her actions. She'd cared for Aquila, too—a lot—but hadn't hesitated to step aside for his burial because she thought it was the right thing to do.

We'd been on and off again as a couple for years, but whichever way the switch had been flipped, we always made it memorable. I'd visited her in the Dominican Republic when she was in the Peace Corps. Living in a hut—three hours from the nearest Guagua bus—that you needed to follow muddy trails or machete your way through the underbrush to reach. The children in the village loved her, everyone there did, and I was grateful to count myself among them in this regard. Skelly's return to the U.S. had come about not long after my relationship with the acupuncturist had ended, and we hadn't just picked up where we'd left off, there'd been serious talk of getting married.

After what happened with Aquila, though, I could barely handle being touched—not by someone who knew the story, anyway—and with our time together becoming less generally effortless, Skelly and I were in a bit of a no man's land as we contemplated the future. I couldn't see moving forward as we had been. And yet I couldn't even conceive of an ending with Skelly, as you don't break up with your best friend—not if you've got a whit of wisdom about you—and it would've made about as much sense as telling Ren I didn't want to see him anymore.

What the two of them offered me, though, was the singular feature that I needed more than any other. The one that had been lacking in all my other intimate relationships, and by definition has to be lacking in any sort of traditional one. Space. As much space as I wanted. The space, even, to become somebody else.

Disappointment in yourself can be lethal, but if you can't overcome it, sometimes the best you can do is put it aside and live to fight another day. Sure, things are bound to catch up with you sooner or later, but it can feel liberating to finally commit to a new direction.

Don't want to give me a job? Fine, I've got other plans. I was free to do what I wanted, and what I wanted was to explore more of the world and more of myself in it.

Hesitant to give sleeping with guys a try? Don't be. It seemed physically impossible I could mess things up any more than I had with women, and it was about time I figured out what the deal was going to be with that. I already knew my dick shouldn't have any trouble getting hard in same-sex situations—thank you, high school buddy incident, for that information. And thank you, too, to every cool non-straight person I'd met since, who helped me to see that fact as a potential strength and not a liability.

Gay? Not Gay? There was only one way to find out. And, really, who was going to be checking my credentials anyway? All I needed was to give myself permission to do what I wanted, and I was ready to grant it.

My birthday was just around the corner.

I knew exactly where I wanted to celebrate.

II. EDUCATION AND EXPERIENCE

A little more than a year later, settled in San Francisco and with my life there in full swing, I'd meet a guy named Daryl. He co-owned a sex club and it was, hands down, one of the best-run businesses I'd seen in operation. They had a system, and the system was you played by their rules or found yourself right back out on the street where you'd waited so long to get in. (Most serious infraction besides not wearing a condom? Wearing a fragrance. Not even a whiff of one was allowed past the door.) That kind of discipline inevitably begins with management, and I credited Daryl for much of their success.

Daryl was by any standard an older man, but never an old man. Guys of all ages would go for him. I can't quite say, "I didn't just consider him an employer, but a friend," because, as Daryl told me himself, he had very few tight friends, all of them outside the business. But he was good to me, he was fair with me, and he would take me into his confidence from time to time. We were setting up one of the dungeons together one night, when he told me his story.

Daryl started his young adult life as both a Marine and a husband, and he remained both until he retired. When his wife got sick, he was beside himself with grief, shed his share of tears, but at a certain point toward the end of her funeral, he made a decision. He told himself he was never going to love another woman the way he'd loved his wife, and in fact was never going to be with another woman again. I don't believe he'd ever messed around with another guy before, but after a respectable period of time, that's just what he did. And he continued to make good on his pledge right up until the day he told me about it.

Certainly, I recognized a number of parallels between Daryl's life and my own. Ones that resonated more than with any other tale of identity swapping I'd heard since arriving in that town. But Daryl had transformed only once. I was just getting started.

SAN FRANCISCO

This could have been another story about a guy going to the big city and sowing his same-sex oats, and there is some of that, but always, in the background at least, is the woman who let me go in the first place. All that freedom I was ragging on about at the end of the last section was given as much as it was taken. Skelly had already agreed to open up our relationship before I left, and even though we didn't talk about the potential of my getting involved with guys, too, it wouldn't have come as a complete surprise to learn it had crossed her mind, considering my choice of a destination. If it did, her take on the whole thing probably wouldn't have been any different than the one she'd taken with women I'd been involved with in the past: "I don't care much about that in general, as long as you don't get involved for too long with anyone in particular." Seeing as those women were no longer in my life and Skelly was, and seeing as I had no intention of getting Involved with anyone, male or female, this approach was on track to work just fine.

Skelly was hardly the stand-by-your-man type. Surely, George F. Will had her in mind when he referred to certain women "having a peculiar abhorrence for [men's] ignorance coarsely expressed."[8] She was certainly smarter than most of them, myself included, as she was smarter than most people. I can't say what it was she liked about me exactly—I was just glad there was something. When I pulled out of town on my motorcycle, I hoped even though I was technically over the age

[8] https://www.washingtonpost.com/opinions/a-loose-brick-in-republicans-red-wall/2020/03/24/349ce6f0-6dee-11ea-aa80-c2470c6b2034_story.html

limit for such activities, she'd view my impending adventures as something of a Rumspringa.

And in the beginning, that's just what it felt like.

Some drunken feel-good bullshit. Some sober feel-good bullshit, too. Getting sucked off while loading up boxes at a warehouse on Hunter's Point, one of my hands still gripping the dolly. Or getting the same treatment at a MUNI stop, a guy strolling up and finding me alone with a book in my hands. Standard San Francisco fare as it turned out, starring in my own mini-pornos, and I played them just like that, mustering up a certain amount of seriousness while the activities were taking place, then smiling to myself afterward. *Well, that sure beats reading while waiting for the train.* There were some awkward moments while pants were down, sure, but what I really cared about was how I felt pulling them back up afterward. Like was there going to be some sort of self-hating, laws-of-nature-breaking, homophobic hangover? And fortunately, for the most part, there wasn't. It didn't feel like I was trying to get something out of my system; on the contrary, I wanted my experiences with guys to become a part of me, wherever things went from there. Thinking back on what had happened with my prep school buddy, I felt like I owned it now.

An early lesson learned was that when some drunk guy gave you his number after he blew you in the bathroom, he didn't necessarily want you to call him the next day. *Who's this?* That'd be me trying to be polite, thinking there was little chance I wouldn't have followed up after hooking up with a woman, but the rules were changing. With women, I'd learned to keep one-night stands to a minimum once I realized I never felt very good about them afterwards—the sex being too far disconnected from deeper feelings—but with guys that same lack of connection didn't seem to matter as much. To them. Or, before long, to me.

I hadn't paid much attention to my looks before, but for a number of reasons, I began to. I don't think I'm being naive when I say that I'd never felt like women had judged too closely on my appearance. Not that I believed they had any problem with it—I'd always figured myself for decent looking with flashes of handsome— but I thought we were all clear on the fact that I was kind of a dork. And even if that dorkiness was increasingly cut with signs of suave as I got older, I'd never really left my roots. Why would I? Confident of where the evening was headed, I rarely missed an opportunity to share the most random thoughts, suggest the most random adventures. The detours were half the fun. Now, as long as I was looking sharp, little else seemed to matter.

I didn't remember this bothering me much until I read over one of the prose poems I'd been working on during this period. After having almost completely neglected my writing during my attempt at a normal existence, I was giving it a try again. I'd ripped up pretty much everything I'd written before and was starting from scratch with little vignettes, determined to get every word right. "Pretty" could just as well have been called "Reflections on My Last Blowjob," and in hindsight, I can see me grappling with what it was like to only register with someone on a physical level. Not a new concept for women, but it was new to me. Maybe I didn't remember it well because it got to seem so normal so quickly, but in any case, it was pretty rich that I was lamenting this focus on my body when, in fact, I'd been the guy spending the time at the gym trying to maintain a better one.

I didn't go out to gay bars very often, but the ones I did try tended to be a bit overwhelming. Practically everyone was a Closer, and I wasn't generally in the mood for that. Sure, the Wafflers were around, but whereas at straight gatherings these guys seemed to compose the majority of the fellas, here they were a much smaller group. In my previous life, I'd been worried I wasn't the most alpha guy in the bar. *Shouldn't I always be on the prowl even if I did have a girlfriend?* Maybe I wasn't, gulp, man enough, and now here I was at gay bars and turning out to be much the same way. Not interested in cruising people, wanting to have a conversation. In practice, this meant I spent a lot of time talking to middle-aged guys sitting at the end of the bar.

Once I'd made some friends in the city, it got better. Then I could check the queer box instead of the not queer one ("You're right, the bartender's hot") and get back to being Guy Number 3, enjoying the company of the people I was with. Like a true Friendster, I'd never get comfortable with the idea of using friends as filler—something to kill time with while checking the room every five seconds for potential hook ups—and if I was really interested in hooking up, I could always go out alone again.

So for a while, it was just the occasional blowjob or handjob, no kissing. But seeing as I was always wanting to push on to the next thing, what I was getting increasingly curious about was fucking. And how that was going to look. Maybe it wouldn't be any different from being with a woman? Or at least not that different. Unless it was very different, in which case a simple Insert Appendage There tactic might not fly. I obviously wasn't feeling hyper-confident about the whole thing, and the more I thought about it, the clearer it became that—sooner or later—someone was going to have to show me the ropes.

Now, older and/or more experienced women have a storied history of showing first-time guys how things are done, and I didn't think it would be too difficult to find their male counterparts. But when you're a guy trying to get with another guy, there are two different ways that information can be imparted, and I realized I was hedging a bit by what I meant by it. Because while there was no record I was aware of of women taking an appropriately shaped object and demonstrating what it felt like to be star receiver (I'd managed to make it twenty-seven years on the planet without knowing what a dildo was), I knew guys wouldn't have to look far to find one.

The only problem was, I wasn't too keen on *that* idea. I didn't really think it would be my thing. But I had to consider the possibility that maybe I wanted a dick in my ass so bad that I'd created a hang-up around it where I was telling myself I didn't want it when really, I did. And seeing as I was trying to liberate myself from as many hang-ups as possible at that point in my life, I finally decided that should be put on the table, too.

I remember the first guy I met who I could've possibly seen giving it a try with. He was a bit older, not on drugs, seemed like a regular guy. He told me he worked in Boston where he was in the health care industry and had a lot of employees under him. Consequently, he came across as mature. And responsible, a huge plus, so I believe for the first time, I asked someone back to my place in the Tenderloin. I didn't leave with him thinking, *Oh boy, I hope he fucks me.* And I didn't really think seriously about fucking him. It just seemed like from the length of time we'd spent talking and the depth of the conversation that there might be something more in the offing.

So he hopped on the back of my motorcycle and I took him home. Maybe it was the motorcycle that did it (the bike's tougher than I am), but when we got inside, he was going on about how much he couldn't wait for me to plow him. It wasn't quite, "I want you to make me squeal like a pig," but it was close enough that I was having a hard time navigating the transition from the mild-mannered manager I'd met earlier. I just didn't feel at all prepared to *possess* the guy like he seemed to want, and in so many words I told him that. Awkward, yes, and even though we did mess around, it was all stuff I'd done before, so nothing ended up getting settled that night. All I knew was that I'd let him down.

Sex was just one of many ways of connecting with the city and the people in it. Even though I wasn't much of a dancer, I went out dancing a lot. To clubs that were always mixed, and I liked being part of the spectrum. I tried Ecstasy for the first time. And, enjoying it very much, tried it again. But not right away.

I remember leaning against a post one night at the End Up, just soaking in the crowd, how beautiful everyone looked, when a guy came up to me, offered me some water, and asked, "You got any more of that stuff?" I looked at him, taking a minute to shake out of where I'd been and trying to understand what he was asking about. Then, when it came to me, I smiled."Sorry, man, I'm not on anything." He looked doubtful so I added, "Really." I hadn't partaken in a couple of months, but it was like once that channel had been opened inside me, it didn't need constant reinforcements to stay open. It still seemed like I was able to see more of people. Feel more of myself. Hear more of the music. I definitely loosened up on the dance floor.

There wasn't a party I was invited to where I didn't go, an offer of coffee with someone I didn't take, a movie I wanted to see that I skipped. I'd come in after dark and set my alarm for an hour or so and then go out again. Under moonlight, I took my motorcycle through that city, under sunlight and fog, back and forth to the ocean, up and down the hills, until there wasn't a street I didn't know. And still I wanted more. But more costs, and even back then, San Francisco was plenty expensive if you wanted to enjoy everything it had to offer.

I'd been working for a used bookstore—a dream job in a number of ways—but the money was crap and I needed to find a way to supplement it. Looking through the back pages of the *Bay Area Reporter*, I compared myself with pictures of the shirtless guys advertising their services, and thought I held up all right. It would mean a lot of cash.

Escorting was another job that seemed like the universe had been steering me toward until I finally took the wheel. I remember a couple months after seeing *My Own Private Idaho* in New Orleans, and a guy across the street from my apartment had chatted me up over a bummed cigarette. He said he'd seen me around the neighborhood, and after not a heck of a lot of transitional sentences, mentioned that I could make a bundle being trade. Before walking off, I told him, in essence, thanks but no thanks, still a ways from the ease I'd feel turning down that guy in the pale-blue pickup. I didn't see how it could enhance my standing with the woman I was interested in at the time (although you never knew with her) but I can't say I was as curt with the idea as I had been with the guy, and the spark of it remained.

In San Francisco, my interest wasn't just in the money. I saw it as an extension of everything else I'd been trying to do. Putting myself in as many different kinds of situations as possible and seeing how I handled them. And then, as anyone who's gotten hold of a piece of paper and a pen with a story on the tip of it would understand, I wanted to write about my experiences. Share them. I was thinking this one might give me a leg up with eventually getting something published and yet, I distinctly remember telling myself to tread carefully. *This is only going to give you more material; it's not going to make the writing better, don't forget that.*

What I should have been most concerned about, of course, was the sex. I didn't have a lot of male on male experience, and I'd be setting myself up for a certain amount of on the job training. But I was spending money faster than I could make it (all it takes is one credit card, thank you Providian), I was impatient, and I didn't want to think about it anymore. I wanted to do it.

Fortunately, the agency I got hooked up with was not only open to hiring someone on the greenish side, but looking to capitalize on it, as there was a portion of their client base that was always interested in checking out someone new to the scene. A big enough portion to provide me with some good writing material, but I never got to find out just how big because it wasn't too long after I'd started taking calls that I was out at a club somewhere on Townsend and the trajectory of my life in the city changed.

The relationships that have stuck with me most over the

years are the ones where I knew I'd fallen for the person the moment we met. With that first serious girlfriend in Georgia, I'd been told a new girl was coming out with us, and when I'd gone up to get her while my buddy turned the car around, I couldn't even put a sentence together when she opened the door. A speechless introduction she long mocked me for. That night at the club, I could feel the guy dancing next to me before I saw him, and when I finally did look over, I thought, *That's it.*

There's not much I can do about the details here: two guys at a club interested in one another, one pretty much sober (me) one pretty much drunk (him).[9] But I will say I'd looked into a lot of men's eyes by that point, and never had anything close to a reaction like this. Until then the stares, while potentially useful, always struck me as something of a gimmick, and whether they resulted in playing around or not, decoupled from any kind of real intimacy. This guy's eyes promised that and more. There was only one distraction, and that was worrying about whether my pager would go off, but by the time he'd climbed onto the back of my bike all I could think about was getting him back to the apartment.

Nick and I got close quick. Holding hands walking down the street, which felt strong and right, little surprises kept for each other in our back pockets, cool conversations, good together in public, better in private. In the bedroom, we took things relatively slow, a little further each time, and that grounded things in a

[9] It was just luck of the draw that night, as Nick hardly turned out to be a lush. He'd been living a straightish life, was there with—minus one person—straight friends, and I just don't think he would've gotten anywhere near me without some significant degree of inebriation.

way that I more than liked. He had even less experience than I did when we met, but within months we were like old hands and I knew that—comparing myself to myself *(read that again, otherwise this is going to come off wrong)*—I'd become the best lover I'd been in my life.

It made me wonder. If some of the oohs and aahs I'd gotten from women in the past had been the result of their indulging me, or maybe just the fact that they didn't know any better. Yes, there was the woman whose tongue would always go ice cold right afterwards and that's gotta be hard to fake, but even with the women I'd had the best sex with, I came to understand it had been the best sex for me, not from me.

Let's face it, when you're first with the ladies, it's exciting but you are completely aware you're in foreign territory there. You're not sure what she's feeling, what it feels like to be touched from her body's point of view. Even if you've read the instruction manual, which I imagine the internet now provides. Everything, everything is ultimately a guess in the beginning, and that's if you're not so excited that you forget about even making a guess about what might make her happy in the first place. I used to think I was all Ricky Suavez because I could stick my dick in and knew where the clitoris was, but let's be honest, I was more focused on my own pleasure than on hers. Something you can get away with when you're twenty. But not so much by thirty and definitely not by forty (affairs ensue).

I imagine some of my more selfish impulses must've been smoothed over by the intimacy I both felt and expressed in a woman's arms, but until then, I'd been unable to import that feeling when I was with guys, making the whole operation something like mechanical. But I didn't fuck Nick, I learned how to make love to him, and that made all the difference.

First, credit goes where credit is due, and that's to Nick (the *New York Times* called him "sultry" on stage and they didn't even get a piece of that). He was just so naturally sensual it couldn't help but rub off a little bit on me. Plus, I wasn't in a foreign country, I was with someone who had a body similar to my own, so I didn't have to read about what felt good or guess what felt good. I knew what felt good. And he, not being in a foreign country either, didn't hesitate to go pretty much anywhere, pouring affection everywhere he went.

I got to the point where I was comfortable with every square inch of my body—even parts that I hadn't been especially fond of before. And once I'd become satisfied with myself— taking my own pleasure as a given, over it for the most part—I became better able to turn that affection back toward him. Realizing how happy I could make him in bed, I began to get off on that more than any physical thing he could possibly have done to me or anything that anyone had done to me before. That's a lesson I should have been able to learn with women, and like most guys, almost certainly would've if I'd stayed on that path, but that's not how it went down.

So if you're a guy and you're wondering how that old guy or that sketchy guy or that French guy is ending up with all the hot chicks, that's why. Paying complete attention to the other person. Even paying attention to yourself if you see that's the thing that's going to get the other person off the most. If you want to take this as my own gay recruiting statement, go ahead, although it's not meant to be anything other than a recounting of events the way I see them. Bottom line: It took being with this guy for me to be fully—yuck, but I'm gonna say it—present during sex.

When you're younger, untenable situations tend to build toward their impossibility rather than announcing themselves as such from the start. You keep cruising along, passing exit ramp after exit ramp, determined to stay on the highway you're on. I'd been back to New Mexico to visit Skelly—she'd been out to see me—and it seemed inevitable we'd end up together again. We always did, and I was willing to believe that no matter what happened in San Francisco, things would sort themselves out along the way. But now, not only was I involved in an increasingly serious relationship, I was having to confront the possibility that I might *really* be gay for the first time.

Until then, it'd been easy. I had a crush on literally half the people I worked with at the bookstore, both guys and gals, and had messed around with both without feeling like anything was on the line. Mercifully, few of them were into labels, either for themselves or anyone else, and I had a brief but utterly joyful period where I didn't feel like I had to define myself. After I met Nick and was wrestling with what that meant for Skelly, I could hear the voices of every one of those co-workers in my head (and sometimes to my face), telling me not to fall for the labels. But the voices weren't loud enough. I couldn't just see it as a decision between two people. One where sex was more likely to come to mind when I thought of the person, and one where simply the idea of being in the other person's presence got the upper hand. It wasn't like these characterizations hadn't come up before, comparing my feelings among various women. And it wasn't like there'd been a bunch of other Nicks out there tipping the scales in that direction. But for some reason, all that history seemed to go out the window, and as far as I was concerned, my entire sexuality was on the line. Looking at the pile-up of broken heterosexual relationships I'd left in my wake, thinking maybe the only thing that had prevented me from being a good long-term partner in the past was that I'd been with the wrong gender, I decided being gay made more sense. I told Skelly that Nick and I were moving in together.

I didn't mention that there were financial considerations, as well, even though the thought of paying half-rent on my apartment had definitely made the idea more attractive. Escorting was supposed to have solved the cash flow problem, but it was hard to see how it wasn't going to create a bunch of other ones if I kept doing it, and as Nick was just working his way into the idea that he might be gay himself, it would have been a lot to ask him to swallow. I can't remember whether I told him about my nascent career that first morning or shortly afterwards, but whenever it was, my initial attitude had been basically, "Deal with it." The more we connected, however, the more I realized I was the one who was going to have to deal with it.

I can't say there wasn't some relief on my end when I explained this to the agency. It had been grinding on me that the guy on the other side of the door *who was paying me* invariably had more experience than I did, and, sooner or later, I would've had to up my game. Now I didn't have to prove that I could. That would make escorting one more thing I'd be quitting without mastering, but even if it wasn't an easy decision, it felt like the right one.

I began to refer to Nick as my boyfriend and somehow the word didn't sound that gay coming off my tongue. It sounded more like the fact that it was. Living together brought us even closer and I just couldn't have been more comfortable waking up next to him in the morning. I liked his friends (even his ex-girlfriend, who did her best to tolerate me), I loved his family (who treated me like I belonged from day one), and even though it was a bit of a battle for us to stay afloat financially, life seemed pretty perfect. But the fact that everything was going along so well should have served as a warning as much as anything else. I'd been there before.

Nick and I were somewhat competitive with each other in a way I hadn't been with any of the women I'd fallen for, but, frustratingly, that was the only difference I could find. And so the night inevitably came with him asleep on my chest as I stared up into the darkness, pretty certain I'd just felt that first tug of tenseness that never boded well. Realizing I could have a future with this guy, I began to feel, among other things, closed in. A little more with each passing day. Right on cue, less than a year after we'd met. *Shit,* I thought, *this may mean I'm both gay and an asshole.*

I was an asshole. Just like with every single meaningful relationship I'd had with a woman, just when everything looked so solid, I began to glance and then finally stare ahead to all those years that would be in front of us if we did stay together, and found the problem or two that I was certain would do us in. Could it really be so mundane that I was just another guy with a fear of commitment?

It sure seemed like it.

There are things that will undo a relationship and if you're getting in deep, you're smart to anticipate what those things might be before you get any deeper. Know your dealbreakers. If you've got a long list of them, you can be sure you're mixing up things you'd like to have with things you need to have, so try to focus . . . on the one or two things that matter most.

I've long since learned the thing that will kill it for me, but in retrospect, the reasons I'd given for backing out of relationships since I was seventeen all the way up to when I was twenty-seven were not these types of key reasons at all. They were challenges, sure, legitimate ones, sure, but they were overcomable with the typical effort you'd expect to make toward anything in your life that you truly wanted to succeed at.

I didn't have this all figured out at the time. I just knew that replacing an F with an M in the equation hadn't affected the result. There was only one other variable left to change and I wasn't sure I could. I didn't want to give up on my relationship with Nick. I was missing Skelly, the only person with who close had never become too close. I loved them both with the full force of my heart, but beyond that unshakeable premise I couldn't see any solutions and I was going into a pretty good tailspin about it.

When I'd first moved in with Nick, Skelly had taken something of a wait and see approach, giving me yet more space and somehow not making it seem like she was putting her life on hold. Now, I was asking Nick to do the same thing. If I couldn't commit to either one of them, maybe I could commit to them both? Nick wasn't too keen on the idea, but with zero experience in such matters and doing his best to find his way, seemed hesitant to issue any ultimatums. We all were. So having spent the better part of a decade being part of a couple—one usually arriving on the heels of another—it would be a decade more before I was in a monogamous relationship again.

NEW YORK

My grandmother told me on more than one occasion that if she hadn't left her heart in Israel, she would have left it in San Francisco. Since I tended to take everything she said as gospel, I'd been prepared to fall in love with the city, but even when that didn't quite happen, I knew our impressions weren't that far apart. I'd more than liked it from the get-go, and with that feeling rarely wavering, I had no plans to leave.

I'd already quit my job at the bookstore to work at Daryl's club after it became apparent that paying half-rent wasn't going to cut it either, and the good money there was made better by the fact that the club doubled as a social outlet. Working late and late-late hours meant that rather than spending a bunch of money going out weekends, it was as if someone was sneaking money *into* my piggy bank at night while I was looking the other way. It also meant waking every morning with the days spread out in front of me, and as those were mainly composed of bike trips, reading, and writing, there was little to complain about. But then one day I got a phone call from my dad, and, as was his nature, he got right to the point.

His office manager had been diagnosed with an inoperable brain tumor or some similarly serious condition, and wasn't expected to make it—either at all, or well enough to be able to stay with the company—and he wanted to know if I'd be interested in coming back to Connecticut to help him out for a while. The most direct answer—*No*—would also have been the one he should've expected, but figuring it was probably just a passing idea he'd decided to throw out there, I softened my response to, "I don't think so, Dad." That's when he dug in.

My father ran a small manufacturing concern, Apollo Molded Products, a spin-off of a family business my grandfather had started back in the fifties, and my father was still partners with my grandfather's original partner. Dad's identity was very much tied up in the business and having just picked up two major accounts in New York, he was feeling a lot of pressure. I sympathized but told him there must be dozens of people he could call who would be better qualified for the job than I was. Dad wasn't interested in my resume, though. What he kept coming back to was the issue of trust and how important it was to have someone around he could count on during this period of upheaval in his company.

We went round and round, neither of us able to make much headway with the other—there might have been one more follow-up phone call where we continued to go round and round—but, in any case, we left it that I'd check in with him one last time about it over the weekend. I made him promise that he'd make some phone calls to other people in the meantime, that he'd think hard on it and see if there was a better way. I made it clear that I'd prefer he didn't ask me again, but I knew if he did, I was going to have a hard time saying no.

It wasn't like my dad had never been there for me before. And it wasn't like I was doing cancer research out in California. I worked the door at a sex club. Or helped out in clothes check, putting people's garments in baskets so they could get naked and play around. Yes, there was the occasional Piss Buddy night (think lots of mop buckets from an employee point of view), but the club was obviously serving a need and trying to do it in a responsible manner and I'd never really questioned the work. That weekend, however, I couldn't help but make comparisons between the nature of the job and what my dad was asking of me, and by the time my shift had ended Sunday morning, I was prepared to let the job go.

I got back to the apartment around 4 a.m., a good time to catch my dad on the East Coast. While his phone rang, I stared at the clawfoot tub in the bathroom, feeling my life in the balance, and when he picked up and said, "I need you," the only question left to ask was, "How soon?" I told him he could count on me for up to a year, figuring that would give him enough time to find a proper replacement, and then we set about making preliminary arrangements for me to get out there.

I suppose this could've been seen as my ticket out of a complicated three-way relationship, but it didn't feel like that. I was already off rock-bottom in terms of feeling torn between Skelly and Nick, and all of us were now clear on what it meant not to abandon someone you cared about even if you didn't have the slightest idea how it was going to turn out with them. I'm sure we each had our own unique misery with this setup—Skelly in New Mexico, Nick in San Francisco, me on a plane heading in one direction or the other—but the connections still felt strong, they seemed to be holding steady, and, personally, I wasn't looking forward to making any further adjustments. But I came to accept—and eventually embrace—the move, as I tended to do once a decision had been made.

If there was ever an environment I felt less suited to thrive in, it was in an office, but after I got settled in, it was good for me to see that the job was just as manageable as anything else. I could, indeed, fit into a collared shirt. It was hard to get overly excited over color samples and inventory sheets, but I did find a meaty project to take under my wing: upgrading the company's computer systems, which I felt better qualified than any of the older staff to handle.

Both my supervisor and my supervisor's supervisor smoked, and I joined them on a regular basis—even though, until then, ninety percent of the cigarettes I'd smoked in my life had been after hours. In the darkness, the flash of a flame or a red-tipped glow could make them seem briefly illuminating, but their overriding attraction was how they just seemed to go with certain people, certain scenes, and now that scenery included breaks and business lunches. For the most part, though, what happened at the office stayed at the office, and outside of it I got to spend quality time with my dad, my grandparents, and the area I grew up in, and overall felt no regrets about agreeing to come.

Nick eventually came back East as well, though it wouldn't be right to say he'd followed me there. Only he knows what part our relationship might have played in it, but he'd been talking about New York for a long time and the main thrust of the move was to pursue his acting career. When I'd met him in San Francisco he'd been a manager at the Y, teaching spin classes on the side and close to letting his acting dreams go, not having done any new productions since college. Now he was determined to make a go of it. Setting himself up in a crackhouse apartment in Fort Greene—needles in the stairwell, bullet holes in the walls—where the front door never locked, and the landlord somehow still saw fit to charge not insignificant rent.

I had endless respect for the risk he was taking. And the hard-fought-for results were tangible: leading roles with a damn good theater company, regular productions, sellout crowds. Off stage, Nick would analyze to the minutest detail what had just transpired on it—not unlike the way I scrutinized every sentence in a book—and we spent lots of time dissecting these types of things together. I didn't really have any other artsy friends, and certainly none who I loved.

It's a big change in any relationship when you're no longer waking in the same bed, and even though I initially stayed with Nick on the weekends when I came into the city, that became less consistent as time went on. I don't feel like either of us made any serious missteps during this time, but separate beds can lead to separate lives and . . . I don't know, really, except that I did mention to him sometime after he'd moved to New York that it didn't make sense for him to keep being exclusive with me. Skelly hadn't. And the arrangement we were trying to pull off was a stretch, although none of us had brought up pulling the plug on it. I can't say I relished the idea of him being with anyone else any more than I had with Skelly, but I was obviously the last one who deserved to have any feelings on the subject, and this seemed like the right step. There was no one else I'd been with and no one I was interested in being with at the time of the discussion, but somewhere inside I must've known I'd be paving the way for that.

The year went by faster than expected. I wrote most nights after work, trying to capture impressions of my time in San Francisco before they slipped away, all the while keeping one eye on the calendar. For different reasons, I imagine my father did the same. When the year was up, though, he didn't try to push me—just reminded me that there would always be a place for me at Apollo if I wanted it— and there were only good feelings between us when we wished each other good luck on my last day. Then I took the train into the city, this time on a one-way ticket.

It wasn't a question of falling in love or not falling in love with New York. It was in my blood. My grandparents had been born there, my father as well, and I knew every address where they've lived in both Manhattan and Brooklyn, including the original location where my great- grandparents had opened their tailor shop on the Upper West Side. They were poor but had tried to make a go of serving wealthy clients in the neighborhood where they lived. My grandmother—the first to put a positive spin on everything—bragged about how they never had to get up from the kitchen table during meals. You could reach the stove, the sink, and the refrigerator from where you sat. The only luxury I ever heard her mention was going to the movies on a regular basis, but that was because the theaters would give the family free tickets if they agreed to put up posters for shows in their shop window.

I'd been visiting relatives in New York since before I could remember the trips. To museums and plays as I got older. This was during the Koch years, so I'd glimpsed the city at its worst, but there'd never been a news story about it that was too deplorable, no shrieking on the subway, nor shot heard round the corner that could take all the shine off that city for me. There was too much else to offset the violence, and like with family,

I accepted the bad parts along with the rest.[10]

I'm trying to think why I'd never once thought of moving there before. I guess it just didn't coincide with the geography of my young adult life, and for many years, maybe it was enough just knowing it was there. But tapping into the city again during my time at Apollo kept my life from feeling like it was falling too far out of balance, and I'd been mostly satisfied just taking the train in and looking around.

If I wasn't staying with Nick in Brooklyn, I was at the Jane Street Hotel in the West Village, notable for having housed the survivors of the *Titanic* after the ship had gone down. The rooms were simple: A desk. A bed. Concrete floors. I'd keep my cold food in the cracked window and felt at home there from my first night.

The hotel was loud, but there was a handful of eerily quiet hours that coincided with the ones when you'd be most likely to sleep. Other than the occasional shuffling to the bathroom, that silence held until the early morning when it was broken by a single hacking cough, soon to be accompanied by a chorus of others, coming through the walls or up the stairwell, the first cigarettes of the day. I told myself if I ever had a kid and

[10] Granted, it's a heck of a lot easier to glamorize something when you're not in the middle of it full time, but there were plenty of people for who the news stories were enough for them to believe the city was irredeemable, and I wasn't one of those people. Having said that, I doubt I would've wanted to raise kids there during that time and I know my grandparents were ultimately happy they'd gotten their young family out many years earlier. Still, that first night in their new home in Connecticut, my grandfather had come in from pacing in the backyard, shaken his head and said to my grandmother, "Babe, all you can hear is crickets out there." Then he'd gone to bed.

they were curious about smoking I'd make them stay there for a couple of nights so they could see how that story turned out. I also promised myself if gargling phlegm ever became my opening move of the morning, then I'd quit.

One of the best features of the hotel was that it was attached to a theater. *Hedwig and the Angry Inch* played there most nights, and there was something about having the city's disparate denizens roll through the front door and right up into the building where I was staying that blurred the lines between life and art. But there were limits on how long you could stay at the hotel, the rooms were first come first serve, and if you got one, even though it was cheapish in comparison with other options, it was never cheap. My financial picture had improved after a year with the company, but what that really meant was wiping my credit card debt clean, not putting money in the bank.

There used to be (and still is, according to my sources[11]) a literary magazine called *A Gathering of the Tribes* and the guy who ran it, Steve Cannon, also operated his apartment as what felt like a kind of flop house for artists. His coolness was of the variety you didn't even bother trying to keep up with, and the fact that he was blind only enhanced his mystique. You were sure nothing was going to prevent him from seeing farther than you. I don't remember exactly how I ended up in his living room, but there I was one afternoon reading him some of my stuff, and as he sat expressionless in his armchair listening, I realized if he'd told me it sucked I would have given up writing right there on the spot.

[11] https://www.poetryfoundation.org/harriet/2018/02/on-steve-cannon-tribes

Afterward we got to talking, and when I explained that I'd soon be leaving my job in Connecticut and was looking for a place to stay, Steve offered me one—sort of. He didn't have any bedrooms available at the time but told me I could share one with a woman who was already living there, her using it at night, and me using it to sleep during the day while she worked. He told me to run the plan by her, and as she seemed cool with it, I began to get excited with the prospects. I was used to keeping unusual hours and liked the idea I'd be fully committed to hanging out with the city at night. It was the right price—chores for a roof over my head—and I was a little starry eyed about the adventures that would surely accompany it.

You file a lot of experience under adventure-taking when you're younger, but you don't necessarily stop to wonder what might be behind it. For me, I think a lot of it had become about wanting to feel comfortable in the world. Not cut off from anything or anyone. Whatever the bed, I could lie down in it. Whatever the job, I could work it. Whatever car stopped to pick me up, I could get inside. A sense of belonging can come from being a part of a group that puts up barriers against other groups to define itself, but to truly feel like you belong on this earth, there's got to be some deeper recognition that we're all in this together. That's a platitude I didn't need to prove to myself, but being attracted to the idea, I did want to prove that I could enjoy it. And, for the most part, I did.

An example of a good night would've been one where I'd left Steve's around dinner and within a matter of hours a guy had picked me up and taken me to a rager[12] on one of those luxury yachts docked in New York Harbor. It was a boisterous affair, the people on it were dressed to the nines, with drinks and hors d'oeuvres in their hands, loose lips, and extended smiles. The guests were just so open with themselves and I don't remember having a bad conversation with anyone on board (plus the food was great). But the image that's stuck with me more than any other is of a group of four or five of us gathered around the hot tub in the wee hours. It seemed like we might've been a range of sexualities, but what we had in common was being special invitees that were not normally part of this particular scene. And this one truly stunning young woman who I'd seen earlier on the arm of a much older man had kicked off her shoes, was dipping her feet in the tub, and when she turned to me her opening line was, "Where'd they find you?" I just loved her for that line. Classic us vs. them, which is oftentimes the easiest lens to see the world through. For me, the yacht was something of a case study in humanity. The intersection of the haves and have nots and have somes. And as dawn began to filter into the harbor, I knew that there was nowhere else I would rather have been.

You're nuts if you think those are the only kind of nights you'll get, though. Most were more uneventful than not, nursing beers, sitting on bar stools or at diner counters, coffee cup refills and 3 a.m. scrambled egg platters eaten at a glacial pace. Cigarette chasers. Walking around, hanging around with people you knew you weren't ever going to see again, writing, reading, nodding off on a bench. Then repeat. In a different order on a

[12] If you don't have a teenager at home, a *rager* is a large gathering of people, maximum action (as opposed to a *chiller,* a smallish group of friends hanging more or less quietly). I stole this directly from our middle boy.

different night. There were never any disastrous nights, although when you're dealing from that kind of deck, you can be certain there's some bad cards lurking in it, and I know I was lucky never to flip one of them (it also helped being close to 6'5 and 200 pounds).

A crappy night wasn't so different from a typical night except I didn't seem to have the same energy for it. The last poetry slam ended, the bar that had hosted it closed. No longer able to absorb words from whatever book I was reading and not inspired to write anything myself, I'd wonder at how I'd managed to get so much more writing done after working a day job. Now, low on sleep[13] and getting lower on cash, I'd think the best thing would be just to find a place to lie down. But then I'd already had a near run-in with what I took to be Park Patrol in Central Park, and it seemed like every hedge that might offer some cover reeked of piss.

I remember looking up at the trees and thinking how much I'd like to crawl up into one of them. Maybe better just to get off the ground for a little while. I'd already noted how the lower limbs on so many had been cut, but then I got angry about it, thinking it was a plot by the City of New York to prevent people like me from climbing them just when they were needed most. And in the hours before sunup the clock ticked by so slow, the same thoughts running through my head, *What are you doing out here? Haven't you done enough of this kind of thing already? You're getting too old for this*, and then circling back to *What are you doing?* again. So that in the morning when I finally walked back into Steve's, it didn't even feel like a relief to discover the

---

[13] My roommate had a cat who seemed to instinctually sense the exact moment when I'd nod off. That's when she'd pounce.

woman I shared a bed with had left early for work. Pulling the blankets over my head, I was too far gone to enjoy it.

It's hard to say where all this bed hopping might've led. I hadn't had any great moment of clarity with respect to my relationships. And career-wise, I was still wrestling with whether writing constituted work, and if it didn't, what the heck else was I gonna do, and if it did, maybe I should adjust my live/work ratio, living less and writing more. The answers would have to wait, however, because it was only a short time later that I learned my dad's plane out of JFK had gone down in the waters off Nova Scotia, and there were no survivors.

After the crash, it was all hands on deck at Apollo. My father's partner had also been on the plane, and his family jumped in with me and the rest of the employees to try to save the business. In between fielding a steady stream of calls from customers and doing my best to reassure them, I took one from a rabbi who was in the process of determining whether my father was entitled to a proper Jewish burial. In Jewish tradition, the body is supposed to be returned to the earth—in its entirety, as it was given[14]—and there was some parsing about whether there would be enough of my father's parts remaining to accommodate this (there weren't). It was somewhere in the middle of this call that an odd sensation crept over me. Like someone had injected a large needle filled with Novocaine into my skull, although I didn't feel the prick. The drug seemed to be pushing through every last part of my body until finally, by the time I'd hung up the phone, I was consumed with it. This happened over the course of maybe

[14] https://www.chabad.org/library/article_cdo/aid/510874/jewish/Why-Does-Judaism-Forbid-Cremation.htm

twenty minutes, but it would be years before it had completely flushed out of my system.

Of course, my personal life took a back seat to all of this. Skelly and Nick remained the two most important people in it, but I was in even less of a position to sustain anything with either one of them. What I said was, "Take me or leave me, this is where I am right now." But what I thought was, *I'm not worth the trouble, you should probably both just tell me to fuck off, once and for all.* Fortunately, that didn't happen right away.

We were all together twice that I remember. Once, at my dad's memorial service, where they had the grace to make it about my dad. And the next time Skelly came to visit, the three of us decided to go out together for a night on the town, something I must have instigated. What was I thinking? Something along the "why can't we all just get along" lines.

I'd spent more than one night sleeping on the office floor next to an overflowing ashtray, and I think I must have just snapped one day and said fuck it. I took my dad's Lincoln Town Car into the city—the one with the skylight that went all the way back—and the early evening began with the three of us driving down Fifth Avenue with that skylight open. One way or another, we'd ended up with a bunch of candy in the car—part of our supply included a bag of, I believe, Tootsie Rolls the receptionist had flung at me when I left the office telling me to lighten up— and at a certain point I had the idea that we were going to throw it out from the skylight to the people on the sidewalk, a few pieces at a time. So we started throwing and sure enough, first one person, then six, then twenty people got the idea and started shouting for the candy, waving, pressing up to the car at red lights. Not like barbarians at the gate, mind you, smiling faces, just playing along, and for a while it was like we were a one float Mardi Gras parade. I loved New York in that moment, like I sometimes do, when I just can't love it any more. I felt the same way about the two people I was with. I even came close to loving myself, and for hours, it seemed like magic continued to happen around us.

We saw the *5000 Fingers of Dr. T* /*The Red Balloon* combo, probably at the Film Forum, and when we walked into the theater they had red and blue balloons taped behind every seat, which we got to take on the way out. Walking around downtown afterward with our balloons in the air, anything seemed possible. We were firing on all cylinders—each of us with the next comment on our lips, just waiting for the first available opening to slide it in and crack us up. They both had a wicked sense of humor, and, with the greatest satisfaction, I realized I could barely keep up with them.

Restaurants, clubs, I'm sure we went. But the last thing I remember is us getting into the car together somewhere on the West Side. It was three, four in the morning, I was about as exhausted as I'd ever been, and I knew I'd need some sleep before dropping Nick off at his place and driving Skelly and me back to Connecticut. There'd been no plans for all of us to stay together and after we got in the car and shut the doors, the utter silence made it clear those plans weren't going to change. I don't think they were trying to give me space—they were both still pretty awake. It just felt like all the fun had been sucked out of the evening and with me no longer capable of keeping a conversation going, they didn't seem to have a single word to say to one another. And I realized as I leaned my head against the steering wheel that they didn't really have a connection and probably never would. They'd both been good sports. And that was all.

At the time, I remember being a little frustrated by it. *Looks like that angle's not gonna work.* Believing the whole evening to have been undermined in the closing moments. But writing about it now, I kind of cheer watching us go through our paces, thinking how many great hours we were able to pull off under trying circumstances. In any case, I didn't have the time to dwell on it. I was due back at the office early Monday morning.

It took a year to bring the business to sale, selling not being a definitive goal but rather a hoped-for one, as none of us thought we were in a good position to run it long term. But the more time I'd worked there, the more I'd become attached to the people and even the problems, and the day I walked into the lawyers' office to sign the papers I was overcome with doubts. Worried my dad would have been disappointed, that this isn't what he would've wanted. *I've been doing all right*, I told myself, *I can keep going.* It took hours for everyone in the room to talk me down.

My partner, who'd known me since I was a kid, took me aside and emphasized how grateful our parents would've been that we'd kept the business from going under. And he also told me not to forget who I was. Neither of us had followed in our father's footsteps, and there was a reason for that. After taking a long walk outside, I finally agreed.

I reminded myself my dad had been looking to merge with a larger company himself—to have access to deeper pockets and a more international market. In fact, the flight he'd been on had been for the purpose of completing such a merger. Accompanied by his business partner, his vice president, and all their wives, they were supposed to ink the deal with a French company and then celebrate in Paris.

There wasn't much celebrating in the lawyers' office that day, but I decided after I'd seen the company through the transition to the new owners, I would go to Paris. To the place my dad didn't make it. I bought a pager, gave the number to a few people, and told them to text me only in an emergency. Then I hopped on a plane.

PARIS FIRST

I'd taken a six-month lease on a flat near Montparnasse, on an unremarkable block where I spent most of my time working alone. It was a luxury to be able to write without working another job or looking for another job or thinking about looking for another job, and I wrote a lot. Keeping track of hours and maintaining a schedule. Seeing as I'd spent most of my life rebelling against normal work hours, it was interesting to see how quickly I put my own in place, once I was fully in charge of them.

Part of my routine included a daily workout at the pool. Every neighborhood had one, and on the days when mine was closed, I'd take the metro to a nearby arrondissement so I wouldn't miss a day. I'd always felt more comfortable in water than on land and I still loved to swim, but the main reason I was so adamant about going was because somewhere over that past year, I'd stopped putting a qualifier in front of my smoking habits ("occasional" smoker, "social" smoker). Now I was just a smoker. And I wasn't about to let myself get Jane Street Syndrome, but I wasn't about to quit, either. It seemed like a bad time to try and an even worse place to do it in. Cigarette smoke hovered over the cafes, came pouring out of bars or restaurants when the front door opened, and with that much already in the air, I figured I might as well enjoy one of my own.

Nicotine can make you justify a lot of things, but I'd managed to never fall totally under its spell before. Eliciting a combination of admiration and disgust from my friends, smokers and ex-smokers alike, with my take it or leave it approach. But there was no reason to be jealous anymore. I was now capable of smoking half a cigarette before I'd even realized I lit it, and that, right there, seemed to miss the whole point of why I'd even bothered smoking in the first place. It should've been something to savor, with company or alone, and still could be, if only I made a point of paying attention to it.

One of my favorite times to light up was after a long hard swim. My lungs must have found it an odd way to commemorate the occasion, but it felt earned, this little bit of pleasure in the pesticides, and at least the inspiration came from something positive. That was true every day I went to the pool except for the first one, when I'd been forced to skip the swim and go straight for the cigarette.

Like with many things in Paris, the public pool experience was a bit of a production. Queuing up to get in, paying the entrance fee, getting your numbered key, then finding the changing compartment that went along with it. By then, I'd decided the building must have been repurposed from something else (I imagined a prison), as each private changing room had its own door, the little changing cupboards lined up next to one another and circling around both the first and second floors with a cavernous open area in the middle that seemed like it would've been a good place to start a riot. Once changed, I walked barefoot across this concrete floor and managed to find the men's entrance, which led through the showers and finally to the pool. I hadn't even had a chance to dip a toe in when the lifeguard started yammering at me.

Unable to comprehend what he was saying, I walked over to him as if maybe the closer proximity would improve my understanding of the French language, but it was still a lot to parse. Something about Oob (which made no sense) and Seine (which kind of made sense) kept cropping up. As he ranted, he gestured to my swimming suit and then to his and then back to mine again and, among other phrases, he kept repeating the sounds together until finally they clicked. *Obscene.*

Now the thing is, I was wearing American style swim trunks. Down to the knee. With a liner. While his threads, well . . .to call them skimpy would have been an understatement; I felt certain the president of Speedo would've been blushing. In a past life, I might have found this all amusing, or at least more amusing than annoying, but at the time, I wasn't in the mood for it. I was pissed. And so, likely feeling freer with my words because I couldn't be sure he'd understand any of them, I went off. *Obscene? Obscene! You wanna know what's obscene? Your fucking ball huggers, dude. No, I don't have another suit. No, you go change. No, you go change.* And so on. With him never making a move to climb down from his high chair and me never attempting to drag him off it. I kept trying to yell over him long after it'd become obvious I'd need to try again tomorrow.

Even though I'd gone to Decathlon and gotten my gear in order, I was expecting more trouble when I went back, but, surprisingly, he acted like nothing had happened. Like so many

French in these types of positions, he'd simply wanted his rules followed, and now that they had been, he took to nodding at me when I'd first walk into the pool area, not unpleasantly. It took a while longer for me to settle into this detente, but eventually I did, and he didn't bother me again.

Stretching-out was just the kind of thing I liked to pass over as quickly as possible when I was swimming competitively, but now, with my body not as flexible as it once was, it seemed like an obligation to do it right. There was a corner of the deck to stretch in that I'd been using for the last couple of weeks and was just in the middle of pulling my elbow back behind my head, when a guy approached me. *What now?*

"There's something about the way you stretch. Like you're showing off your muscles."

I stared at him, bug eyed. And I didn't even have my goggles on yet.

"C'est un peu arrogant, non?"

"What are you talking about?" I'd already had some practice trying to defend myself at the pool, but still, it took a moment to fully compose a response. Feeling, somehow, like I owed him one. "I'd do it the same way if I was the only one here."

He looked into my eyes, serious as I was. "But you're not the only one here."

I sensed some deeper truth in that but wasn't about to investigate it any further. *Of course, I wasn't the only one there.* "C'est tout. Is that all?"

He nodded.

I pulled my googles down over my eyes and got into the pool. *What was it with these French guys?* I couldn't have told you the first thing about anyone else who'd been using the pool except, as a group, they tended to take their time in the lanes and made passing difficult. The lifeguard, at least, had been doing his job. Who went and made this guy assistant pool monitor? And I'd cut my stretching short as a result of his coming up to me, I didn't like that one bit. I tried not to remember exactly how handsome he'd been, but despite having pushed my laps and snapped every single one of my flip turns, he was still on my mind when I ran into him again in the showers.

"I didn't mean to offend you," he said, and this time he smiled.

There's a time between knowing you're going to sleep with someone and when you actually do that's worth extending if you can manage it. Anticipation's half the fun, and it seemed like all the time I spent with Cedric in the following weeks was composed of it. That afternoon, we went out to grab a bite to eat, and I noted with some satisfaction that the first thing he did when we sat down was light a cigarette.

The ensuing conversation was pleasant enough—we shared our views on the world—but it never felt like anything was at stake with our words. I noted in real time the way I argued against but ultimately discarded things he said that I didn't necessarily agree with while glomming on to those that I found more attractive. His English was good, better than my French at least, but it didn't need to be. We were just taking each other in.

Afterwards, he came back to my apartment for a coffee and then, at the door, a kiss goodnight. I could still taste him in my mouth after I shut it, trying to digest both how quickly it had all happened and how my working theory that Nick would be the only guy I'd ever fall for had just been put on the chopping block. I loved how what I was feeling seemed so far removed from the rest of my life, how it didn't seem like anything could touch it. And that feeling only deepened the more time we spent together.

Cedric was in his mid-twenties and could've been getting laid every night by a different guy if he wanted, but that's not how he rolled. There'd been an older guy he'd spent most of his young adult life with. Another guy he'd seen briefly after that. And supposedly that was it. Even though there was likely some arrogance of his own tied up in this, I respected him for it. We all have strategies for protecting ourselves, and his suited him particularly well.

Cedric worked some kind of regular job, but he'd been going through the lengthy process of applying to be a steward on Air France—apparently a big deal as they only took a handful of new hires each year. He'd made it down to the final cut and believed his chances were good.

I liked how his life seemed full when he was apart from me, and then how it retreated into the background when we were together. I wrote well during this time, tamping down my emotions just enough to make my writing hours, and spent the rest of the time looking forward to seeing him. Our dates were getting increasingly intimate, but one night he arrived at my apartment seemingly preoccupied with something, and after some small talk, made clear what was on his mind.

"I want to make love with you tonight."

There wasn't going to be any arm twisting on that front—we'd drawn it out long enough. But I couldn't be sure if he was just waiting for the idea to sink in or whether he had something more to say.

"I have to ask you something, though."

Uh oh. "Okay." I said slowly. *Maybe he just wanted to know my HIV status.*

"Are you really free? Free to be with me."

Free? Only the French can get away with tossing off some existential question like this and have it sound in any way reasonable; I couldn't pretend I didn't know what he was asking about. Until then, I thought I'd done a decent job of navigating around my personal life, listening while he shared his own story, then circling back and asking him more questions rather than sharing mine in return. I imagine I must have dropped a few obtuse comments along the way, but otherwise it hadn't felt like I'd been trying to hide anything so much as I'd found myself with little desire to talk about my past. He hadn't pressed me until now, and I was kicking myself for not having used the time to prepare better.

"Well," I started in, "I've kinda got a girlfriend . . ." and I explained a bit about Skelly. Not exclusive, no. Same with the kinda boyfriend. Nick. I started to explain a little bit about him, too, but I was already feeling off about it, not just because of the way Ced was looking at me, but listening to my own words, said aloud, for the first time. It was sounding increasingly dubious and I hadn't even gotten to the part about how I'd gotten involved with a woman before leaving Apollo. Our lovemaking had felt intense and necessary, a result, no doubt, of dealing with the fallout from the plane crash. But she was married. And when her husband had called me up shortly before I left the States to talk about it, I knew I was in over my head.

I'd gotten briefly lost in my thoughts when Ced put his hand on my thigh. "I'm sorry, but I can't see you anymore."

Wait. He was getting up from the bed. I couldn't believe he was going to leave. My mind was racing trying to come up with just the right phrase that would fix everything. But there wasn't one. I watched him grab his coat, and then, when he reached the door, turn back toward me. His eyes were filled with tears, but his voice was steady when he spoke.

"I really thought I could have something with you. But you're dangerous." And then he left.

To avoid confronting the profound sadness I felt at this departure, I occupied myself by picking apart the reasons for it. *Dangerous?* That was more than a little dramatic. I was just being honest. People's lives were complicated, welcome to the world, kid. And he barely gave me a chance to put anything in context. What did it matter what I left behind in the States, that was an ocean away and I was here now. But there was a point where I couldn't hold out against the accusation any longer, and that's when I started to consider the ways it might actually be true.

I thought of discussions with Skelly or Nick that hadn't gone well. When it had been clear they were unhappy, and I'd been unable to deny that I was still taking up real estate in their hearts that could otherwise have been built on. I thought about the mess that had been unleashed with the woman at work. Her family. How I hadn't thought through any of the repercussions in advance. I thought about other entanglements along the way where, despite my best intentions, the other person had gotten hurt, and I realized this guy was probably right to get ahead of the curve. *Why would this time be any different?* There seemed to be no end to the directions I could go with this theme, and, thinking about my relationships more broadly, I finally considered the one with my father.

When Dad was still in the process of trying to woo the French company, he'd become quite the World Cup aficionado, bringing a mini television to the office so he could keep up with the matches. He knew how important soccer was to the other president, and stretching the limits of my high school French, I'd worked some commentary about it into the closing of a letter he'd asked me to help draft about the potential deal. My father knew I was an ally in this venture. There were others—within the company, in the family—who were cool on the merger idea, but I believed it was a good move for my father. To help relieve some of the pressure he'd been under, to have someone with larger resources to back him up. Of course, that's what I told him when he'd asked my advice, but that hadn't turned out so well, and even though I'd made this connection before, it was the first time I allowed myself to really go in on it.

Dangerous.

I hardly slept that night.

The next day I was supposed to give a hand to a guy I'd gotten friendly with in my building. He'd moved his family from Guadeloupe to try to find a better life in Paris, and they'd had me down to dinner, over for beers, every time spent together a good one. For my part, I'd meet him at the school gym on the outskirts of the city where he coached a kids' basketball team and help run drills, do quick demos, whatever he wanted me to do. He was an excellent guy and there was no chance of my not showing up.

That didn't mean I thought I'd be of any use that day, but the practice was a good distraction, the kids making the world seem like it was a better place than it really was—*Dunk it again, Monsieur, dunk it again*—and I was able to carry some of that good cheer back to the station with me. But I'd already slipped back into the funk I'd been in even before I boarded the train.

For much of the ride, I stared out the window. But as we got closer to the interior of the city, I looked around to see how close we were to my stop and noticed a guy staring at me. *Oh, come on.* I felt like growling. While he, having caught my eye, seemed to be doing everything short of waving his arms to show that he wanted some sort of further attention. I tried to ignore him, but could still feel his eyes on me, so I gathered the full force of my feelings together and glared at him. With the single worst look I'd ever given a stranger. *Don't you see I'm poison, you idiot? Leave me alone.*

And what did he do in response? Smiled. Not stupidly, but resiliently, as if he were impervious to my anger. Which only made me angrier, so I put my best *What the fuck?* into the shrug I gave him and turned away.

Longer-term changes in your personality tend to show up first in short-term ways. A cough here, a sneeze there, before you realize you might really be coming down with something. My anger had generally been slow to boil, if it ever boiled over at all, and this reaction had felt so close to the skin. With a stranger, of all people, the one type of person I had a near-perfect track record of treating well. Once I'd simmered down, I couldn't decide whether I liked this version of myself better, but I did know it scared me a little. When my stop came, I gave the guy a quick nod on the way out, hoping it would be taken as *Sorry.*

I can't say I was completely surprised when, walking away from the metro station, I felt a tap on my shoulder. It was the guy from the train, wanting to know about getting a coffee. He still had that hopeful grin on his face. And I didn't have any reserves left to take anything else out on him. "Sure," I said, "why not?" Agreeing to the coffee. And, eventually, to having a best friend in Paris, something I wouldn't have guessed I needed.

As you get older, it gets harder to make friends. Good ones, I mean. There's less of a desire to try, first of all, as there's so much to have to explain to catch someone up and it rarely feels like it's worth the time, yours or theirs. I'd just turned thirty and Yoan was about to do the same and we talked about what that did and didn't mean to us. We talked about our parents' divorces. The effect that'd had on us growing up, being the older sibling. Unlike the first conversation I'd had with Cedric, the topics were almost all personal, but I answered whatever questions were asked of me, figuring I didn't have anything to lose. At a certain point, Yoan told me he was gay, which I hadn't quite felt on the train, and still wasn't feeling it.

"So you were just trying to pick me up?"

"I didn't think you were gay. But I knew you were American." He pointed at my baseball cap. "And I've always wanted an American friend."

"Hm . . ." I hesitated. "Well, I can be gay," I told him, "but don't get any ideas." And then I added, using a line for the first time but not the last. "I'm not boyfriend material."[15]

When I left Paris many months later, on my way to the airport and watching the city give way to the banlieue, the banlieue to

[15] Gaydar, already suspect in most environments, is pretty close to useless in Paris. Almost every guy seems like he *could* be gay, almost no guy seems like he necessarily *is*.

the countryside, I realized my biggest romance had been with the city itself. I'd known enough French to get by, to express any simple idea or ask any question, and I could understand any simply (and slowly) worded answer in return. But the rest of the time, the voices were a blur. Background to an old city—its buildings, its statues, its streets endlessly sublime—its history whispered wordlessly in any ear that took a moment to listen.

I didn't have to say anything back, of course. The city was indifferent to my story, no detail too off-putting or intriguing. There was no chance of my charming Paris, and so I found myself holding nothing back. Allowing a depth of emotion that had become dangerous to plumb. Standing under a streetlamp in a cobblestone alley, half in shadow, a cigarette burning at my side, I'd look around and feel utterly unique in my admiration, while also knowing there had been and would continue to be countless other admirers long after I'd gone.

BACK TO THE STATES

When I returned to the States, it was to places that I was drawn, and places that I set up my life around. New Mexico and New York. The forest and the big city. Antidotes to one another.

Even though I would sell the land where Aquila was buried, I purchased another piece from a man who'd bred and raised wolves on it. He fed the legend that a few of his hybrids had escaped over the years and mixed in with some of the wild dogs and coyotes that roamed the area, forming a ghost pack. One you would never see, only hear howling in the distance.

I had plans for the property but it needed taming: the trees thinned, brush cleared, a fire line put around the perimeter as it was surrounded by National Forest. Like most tracts granted under the Homestead Act, this one was a quarter mile by a mile, and there was something in the vastness of the project that appealed to me. I worked alone, with Ren, and, once the pine beetle had returned to New Mexico, with a crew. Under a grant from the Forest Service which—as the beetle began to spread—was increasingly fearful there wasn't going to be any forest left to service.[16]

We were in the epicenter of the outbreak, and there were few daylight hours we didn't work, bucking the infected trunks, placing them in plastic solar ovens we'd made to bake the beetle,

---

[16] I won't subject you to the whole article the Forest Service had me write up but the gist of it is this: Pine beetles are part of the forest ecosystem; they help break down what's already rotting on the forest floor, but in times of drought they rise up out of the slash to attack healthy trees. Normally a tree can handle them just fine: a curious beetle tries to drill under the bark, a healthy tree saps it out. But we were experiencing the worst drought since the 1950s, the trees were too dry to make sap, and that left them defenseless.

The pine beetle is no bigger than a fraction of your fingernail and yet all it takes is one to make it into the cambium and inject a blue fungus that will destroy the life processes of the tree. Then it puts out a pheromone to call its friends over to feast—on the young and old alike—and suddenly trees that were supposed to be future forest, or ones that had been around for hundreds of years, become nothing but fire hazard. The needles will eventually turn a sickly orange, but before that happens you can see just the slightest fade to the green, and even though the tree appears otherwise normal, you know it's already dead.

I hadn't really cried since Aquila was shot, and it would be many years, still, before I would cry again, but that first July 4th, I woke up to a beetle infection that, despite our best efforts, seemed to have doubled overnight, and my eyes filled with tears. Looking up at the sky, at stray passing clouds that refused to gather, I thought, *There's no hose big enough in this world to water the forest. Please rain.*

then chipping the infected branches, sometimes under headlights or the moon. But usually sundown would find us with freshly popped beers in our hands, me with a chew in my mouth instead of a cigarette, looking out over the valley we'd just worked and noting both the sections where we'd temporarily stopped the beetle's advance, and the ones that had been conceded for another day.

When the cold weather came and the beetles were forced to overwinter under the bark, in the stumps we'd left and even along the stump roots under the dirt and snow, I hung up my chainsaw and headed for New York. Temporarily reclaiming the studio I'd sublet and insuring that, between my coming and going, I was never around anyone for very long.

Skelly was still living in New Mexico, but we'd finally hit an obstacle we couldn't overcome. She wanted kids. I still wasn't ready for that. The more she pushed the idea, the more I pushed against it, and when the day finally came that she told me she couldn't wait any more, the best I could console myself with was the fact that there'd been a New Mexico before Skelly and there would be one after. Not unlike the way I figured New York wouldn't change just because Nick had decided to move back to California. There was a vague sense that things were getting away from me, but seeing as I'd come back to the States determined to simplify my relationships, maybe things were just falling into place.

As it was, I wasn't feeling like the nicest guy anymore. My patience was getting shorter, my temper quicker, and I'd attained a level of judgment around other people's problems that I'd never known before, finding most of them trivial and therefore easy to dismiss. My theory that I'd been born with an empathy gene wasn't holding up so well, and I wondered what other qualities that I'd previously thought of as intrinsic were up for debate. My faith in a higher power wasn't one of them, but I was losing faith in my ability to deal with the universe that I believed that higher power had created. Not being one to question why bad things happen to good people hadn't meant I'd been able to embrace the idea, and there'd been plenty of opportunities to try in the time both before and after the plane crash.

I'd had a good friend murdered, another take his own life. A new friend plummet to her death off a balcony when she got locked out of her apartment doing laundry.[17] There'd been cancer diagnoses. One fatal. Another merely devastating—a cousin I was particularly close to facing endless treatments at the hospital. And somewhere in the middle of all this I managed to lose my grandparents, my grandmother above all others the person most responsible for showing off the world in its best possible light. In the time between my first memory of her—in her backyard, throwing me the baseball—and the last—when she squeezed my hand one final time before slipping away—I'd come to believe that if only you had just one person in your life

[17] When her mother called me up right after it happened—having found my number in her backpack and looking for any kind of connection to her daughter's life—it was a full two and a half hours on the phone together. Early on in the conversation, I tried to explain I'd only known her daughter for a couple of months, but that didn't seem to register in any important way, and so I spent the rest of the phone call mining every moment of the time we had shared—for stories I hoped would bring a knowing smile to her face, or make her proud, or back up points that she wanted to make about her daughter's character. I could tell she was afraid to get off the phone, so we continued to talk well into the night, but ultimately she was looking for answers I didn't have.

who loved you unconditionally then you were bound to make it. But she wasn't around anymore.

It was feeling like nothing less than a slaughter of people I loved, people I cared about. And I was feeling impaled just on the point where two competing impulses crossed. One, that I had some sort of right to be a little depressed, be a little sad, be a little out of it, and the other, its opposite—frankly, its stronger opposite—that I had absolutely no excuse whatsoever to be a little depressed, a little sad, a little out of it. Because I was alive and well, thank you very much, and believed I should've been nothing but grateful. But being grateful can feel like its own kind of betrayal, and I couldn't come to any peace with either the dead or the living.

Haunted people don't necessarily come with warning signs, however, and I was just as capable of being pursued as anyone else. The number of entanglements I was juggling should've been getting whittled down, but it seemed like every time one person dropped off the roster, there was another waiting to take their place. I realize no one can live up to the kind of publicity that's being implied for myself here, and I don't claim to. As I've already mentioned, I wasn't the smartest nor the best-looking guy around. But not everyone will walk away when they sniff trouble.

It's not enough to say some people are into challenges. Challenges are things people usually engage in with the larger purpose of overcoming them, not because they like knocking their head against a wall. A bunch of walls, really, assuming that's what you've surrounded yourself with. Not willing to accept the bleakest scenario—that you're hollow inside and going to stay that way—maybe they believe if they keep knocking, a crack will open up and suddenly there will be all that space to rush in and fill.

In any case, I kept getting involved and it kept happening in the same way. An occasional hookup with a guy that was never meant to go anywhere and didn't, and the occasional hookup with a woman that always turned into something more. The evidence was overwhelming at this point and it was past time to do something about it.

SYLLOGISM

Do you happen to know what a syllogism is? Well, first of all, it's something that's gonna get us the heck away from all that depressing material from the last section (don't worry, we'll be getting back to sex momentarily). But basically, it's an argument in three parts, where two statements which are assumed to be true lead to a conclusion. I'm using a loose definition because I'm giving a loose example, but I was strict about following it at the time. It went like this:

A. I didn't want to get involved with anyone else.
B. I would be much less likely to get involved with men than women.
C. Therefore, I would only mess around with men.

Easy enough to understand, right? But also easy to poke holes in, so let's get pokin'.

The most obvious reason to be skeptical about this plan begins right there with Concept A. Not wanting to get involved with anyone else. Not that it wasn't wildly true, but a valid premise doesn't necessarily justify its conclusion and there was an obvious angle to take where I was gayer than I was willing to admit and would have used any old excuse to get down to Concept C, sleeping exclusively with guys. And while it's certainly worth acknowledging this possibility, it contains a chicken and egg problem that I'm still not in a position to solve. That is, were my mental desires informing my physical ones, or was it the other way around? In the end, I'm not sure it really mattered. I was gay enough.

Like Concept A, Concept B held up pretty well on its own. I'd proven I was much less likely to get involved with men. So much less that there'd only been one and a quarter exceptions: Nick and the guy in Paris. But Nick was a big exception. He'd ended up in therapy to try to "distance himself from the relationship" (apparently the three thousand miles weren't enough) and given the *reasons* why I didn't want to get involved with anyone else—that I wasn't cut out to be a heartbreaker, that I didn't want to hurt anyone else—then you might appreciate how much I was looking to avoid a repeat performance. Still, I'll admit to a willingness to accept more potential casualties with guys. And to some old-fashioned thinking about men and women that helped explain it.

Now old-fashioned thinking is sometimes superior thinking and the world would likely not be going to hell quite so quickly if we followed more of it. But the rest of the time, old- fashioned thinking is just backward thinking under another name. When it comes to the differences between men and women, you can decide which category this one falls into, but in the spirit of my natural biases, let's let the ladies go first.

It wasn't like I felt like women deserved better, exactly, but that they deserved more of something. . . attention, care, I guess. Now, in some circles, that kind of thinking could be a sign of gayness itself—too sappy—while in others it could be considered chivalrous thinking, and in still others, sexist thinking. In any case, it was my thinking. Women's suffering tended to bother me more.

Maybe it was because since the dawn of civilization women have taken more of the crap and I felt like they already had enough on their plates. Maybe it was watching my mom suffer through the divorce. Maybe it was having a younger sister who I loved (and love) very much, and when you've seen the hurt that happens on the other side of things when guys behave callously, that's always going to be there in the back of your mind. So, yes, I was guilty of thinking that women—while far from being helpless—could use a bit more protection. And more importantly, I was convinced they needed protecting from me. Especially moving into my thirties when I met women all the time who I was pretty sure would sleep with me but feared that underpinning that flirting was a desire to settle down and start a family before it was Too Late. I couldn't have a conversation for more than half an hour without a comment or two reminding me of that fact, and yet if I'd really been ready for that sort of thing, I would've already settled down with Skelly.

Were there women out there who just wanted to have sex? Definitely. But I can't pretend in the name of gender equality that the numbers were similar, because they weren't even close.

With guys, I'd had a decent amount of evidence that they were just fine with having NSA sex and, as it turned out, I'd only gather more. Even if you cut out half the guys who say they only want sex—guys who claim that's all they're looking for but are actually looking for something more—that still leaves a lot of guys in a big city who are really after what they say they're after. A quick hello and goodbye. It's not that men can take care of themselves better than women—please—it's that people who have realistic expectations tend to get hurt less than people who don't.

And that leads to the final issue with this syllogism, which is that you might have noticed there's something cold in my thinking that permeates the entire thing. The idea of making a calculation out of my personal life, as if it was a logic problem to be solved rather than a decision that would be affecting other people's lives. This one's easy to address because of course there was something cold in my thinking because there was something cold in my thinking toward everything and everyone during that period of my life. I don't think cold thinking necessarily makes you a bad person. I just think it makes you less of one.

THE BIG FOOTNOTE[18]

[18] The person I'm in the process of describing doesn't exist anymore either, so there's no need to send me a Bible (I already have one) or give me your psychiatrist's number (my sister's a therapist, we talk plenty) or be envious and feel like you need to compete (you're probably going to anyway, but try to keep it to a minimum).

This is particularly true in the Mr. Studly department. Yeah, I got around a little, but keep in mind, I'm past my prime as I write this. Not only that, I sustained a pretty unpleasant injury a number of years back. It involved an unsettling snap, blood, and even though I mostly healed up, I managed to permanently zap some nerves down there during that little frolic, and I don't feel as much as I used to. If I were still capable of having as much sex as I once did, I'd probably be in someone's bed right now, not crapping around trying to write about it.

I've also gotten much more conservative in terms of my general risk-taking behavior, as there's a tendency to do after you have kids. This point was recently driven home when my little girl and I were reading through all the Harry Potter books and she asked me what house I thought I would've been in if I went to Hogwarts. I wasn't sure, so we looked up more specific descriptions online and I had her read them to me. That's when I realized I'd become a frickin' Hufflepuff. (And not only that, my second option would've been Ravenclaw. We ended up deciding if we went to the school, we'd have formed our own house, Huffle-Claw.)

I debated about whether to mention that I used to be a something of a Gryffindor. Bold, reckless. I was more proud of it than not, as it requires a certain type of confidence to pull this kind of thing off and I liked having that confidence. But pride rightly goeth before a fall, and I fell down more than once, each time wondering if this was really going to be the best I had to offer.

I wasn't going to go into all that with our daughter, of course, because that would have required me to differentiate between the things I was proud of and the things I wasn't, and that would have been too much information. More than I thought she was ready to hear, or at least, more than I was ready to give. But the discussion had made me acutely aware of the surprise she would inevitably feel when she learned more about me, so I decided to take a first crack at tempering it. Saying something along the lines of, "I may be a Huffle-Claw now, but just know your Daddy wasn't always like this."

I should've seen it coming, but what was meant to be both an opening and closing statement led to questions about what exactly I meant, and I had to put it in reverse pretty quick to get us back to Harry and friends. The few words I'd already shared had sounded enticing enough, and that wasn't the impression I wanted to leave her with, as there are clear and definable ways you don't want your kids to turn out like you.

THE RULES

The syllogism was fine in theory, but it wasn't going to work very well in practice without some ground rules to back it up. So I came up with a bunch of them. Probably just the ones you'd expect, including:

No commitments beyond the next hour or two.

No second dates.

No phone numbers exchanged.

No sleepovers.

No sleeping at all, if possible, although I did doze off a time or two.

I can remember times waking with the room brightening around me and—still committed to my vow to always leave before the sun came up—grabbing my clothes and running out the door like a freaking vampire. Pressing elevator buttons or racing down someone's stairs, then out onto the street where I tried to get my bearings so I could work my way back to my apartment in the East Village, a basement studio that shared a wall with the boiler room and was easy to keep in complete darkness.

Having lots of random sex is hardly the default response to circumstances such as the ones I found myself in. But it's an option. Faced with the likelihood that I was going to be alone for a while, maybe a very long while, maybe forever, I knew I was still going to need some kind of human connection beyond friendship. And while some of my desire for sex could certainly be attributed to simple friskiness, I don't think it was just that. There was the adventure. The bit of connection that went along with it. And it did still mean something to me to try to make another person happy, even if it was only for a little while. Maybe it's pouring on too much moral window dressing to put it like that, but if you can remember how you felt the last time you put a smile on someone's face, it shouldn't be that difficult to understand what I'm talking about.

There were other ways I could've helped out the community, of course. Baking someone a casserole, for instance, and bringing that over instead of whipping out my prick every time I walked in the door. But let's face it, I wasn't a cook and had even less patience in the kitchen than I did anywhere else. I wanted to play to my strengths, which are only worth measuring once you've subtracted your weaknesses from them, and if I was destined to be Mr. Wrong long term, I could at least get temporary Right Guy status for an hour or two.

From here, you might see how it wasn't that big a leap for me to get back into escorting again. It wasn't like I'd been biding my time, exactly, but there was something unfinished there and it seemed like the right time to pursue it. I didn't have any other commitments, the money would be nice but not necessary, and the sex part I could have done blindfolded by now (and, in fact, was offered that opportunity by one of my first prospective clients). I just had to work through the initial challenges of getting myself set up online and overcoming my general ineptitude on the phone. Then I could focus on the experience, one I felt well adapted to and hoped to incorporate into what I was writing at the time. I hadn't accumulated enough material from my first go-round, and then, by the time I did, there were other reasons to keep doing it.

First of all, I liked the simple transactional nature of it. Clients rarely tried to push my boundaries, and the boundary

I cared about most was the one they never pushed. I wasn't boyfriend material, and both parties knew it was an arrangement, not a date.

I was nicer as an escort. With clients, I didn't have to come up with some explanation for why I had to leave so quickly afterwards. My departure was already scheduled and, knowing that, I rarely kept a close eye on the clock. Instead, I could pass time with someone who I hadn't been picky about choosing, not caring about the last time they went to the gym.

Sure, I was playing a role, but it was one I often preferred to the person I was in the rest of my life, and in some ways it felt more genuine, allowing me to express parts of myself that I'd become shy about putting on display. Kindness—when I'd been able to manifest it—had become a kind of curse with me. Showing too much led people to believe I was a better person than I was, someone they thought they'd like to have around more. Which was helpful for repeat business, but outside of the escorting arena it could lead to complications I didn't want. Because there were still that other fifty percent of men out there who, despite what they'd said on their profile or when I'd first met them at the bar, really did want more than one-time sex, and I could never tell who was going to be who in advance. Which meant when I wasn't working, I was always in danger of breaking my own rules.[19]

[19] If I really wanted to avoid these types of complications, I obviously would've stuck with escorting full time. Or at least made sure it composed the majority of my encounters, which it didn't. I thought about it, but there were other considerations, and, like with hooking up in general, I wanted to do it on my own terms.

THE EXCEPTIONS TO THE RULES (Stateside Edition)

The first case is pretty self-explanatory. A hookup turned into a friendship and that friendship was worth keeping.

In the second case, a hookup turned into a scattered few more. This was with a kid. And when I say kid, I mean mid-twenties. Even though I wasn't much into twinks, there's always someone to come along and cause you to rethink what you're into, and the way I handled those situations was to card a guy before following through on any action. *Let me see some ID . . . Seriously.* Not like twenty-one is some sort of magical demarcation line between boy and man, but there were so many guys out there and it was like why not at least entertain the illusion I was holding on to some standards. Anyway, this kid was puppy-dog nice, trying to put himself through law school, plenty busy himself, and he just seemed to instantly comprehend the limits of my situation. So when he asked that first night how I'd feel about him checking in from time to time, I was like, let's give it a try. He was pretty much perfect on his end. Months would go by and not a word, no chitchat emails or texts to be obligated to answer, and then, out of the blue, hey are you in town this week, do you have a little time? And I'd be like, yes I am and yeah, I do.

I wouldn't call him a fuck buddy because the messing around was too infrequent and we weren't really buddies. But because he was so understanding about the whole thing and wanted so little, I always enjoyed being with him, and in the end, imagine I got every bit as much out of our time together as he did.

I did give the fuck buddy thing a go with another guy. That would be Finn, exception number 3. To give you an idea about him, one night I was at his place watching *The Daily Show*, feeling feverish, and would probably have burned up right there on the couch if he hadn't insisted on getting me to the hospital. I agreed to go after the show had ended. My leg had gotten torn up back in New Mexico working in the forest, and along with the injury, I'd brought along an infection. What I didn't realize was I'd failed out of my antibiotic, and by the time I got to the hospital, my temperature was pretty off the charts. Once the doctors got that under control, Finn was able to come in during visiting hours and, God bless him, gave me a hell of a celebratory hand job under the bedsheets.

Considerate guy, he was. Well-liked by everyone. He had a ton of friends and it was easy to understand why. I really dug that he was someone I would have been pals with under any circumstances at any point in my life, and here he was bringing along some notable fringe benefits at just the right time. What clinched it for me, though, was his accent. He was the one Scottish guy working in the oldest Irish pub in Manhattan, and every time he opened his mouth it was like, blah blah blah, while all I heard was sexy sexy sexy. I never got tired of hearing it.

He did test the limits of my abilities in bed, however. More so than any client I ever had. When we got together, he had me going rounds like I was seventeen and every time he convinced me I was up for another one, I had to laugh to myself, thinking, *Careful what you wish for.* Because, hospital rooms aside, I was long past the point where a hand or blowjob was going to cut it for me personally, and when say I was looking for sex, I was generally looking for the whole shebang.

SOMETHING OF AN ASIDE

If you've been reading your Savage columns, you know that not all guys who sleep with guys fuck. The possibilities are pretty much endless and plenty of them don't end up with someone's dick in somebody else's ass and that bears repeating here. Having said that, once you've established there *is* gonna be dick in ass, the next question to answer is whose junk is going to be in whose trunk. Top or bottom?

It kind of impresses me that these terms have entered the standard lexicon. That most everyone, gay or straight, knows the deal. Growing up, the main thing I heard about gay men's proclivities in the bedroom was that they stuck gerbils up their butts, which made the whole thing seem unreal, like someone sharing a ghost story around a campfire that gave you a quick shudder but nobody should've believed. The top/bottom designations only get partial credit for accuracy, however, as they don't represent any kind of definitive geographical location for either of the persons they're being attributed to, so you have to wonder what else is being implied.

The equivalent French words—*actif* and *passif*—could shed some light on the subject, and we should at least shed it for the benefit of certain Americans in Paris who might not otherwise understand what's being referenced in a given conversation. (Americans like me who, after being asked if I was actif/active, responded, "Oui, bien sûr, j'aime jouer des sports—Yeah, of course I'm active, I like to play sports." So you owe me one if you're now able to avoid this minor embarrassment.) But beyond that, the French terms further illuminate the American ones by hinting at something that many people think of as true but really isn't: Bottom = passive = your turn to be the girl this time.

First of all, plenty of bottoms aren't passive at all. They're giving out as much as they're getting within the confines of whatever particular position you happen to have them in, or they've put themselves into. And if that position happens to be on the ground on all fours, so be it. The idea that this somehow makes a guy desperate—when, to the extent there is any desperation involved, it's just as likely to accrue to the top who's looking for a place to put it—is pretty absurd. But if there is one sexual act between consenting adults that's got more stigma attached to it than any other, it's gotta be a guy who's getting plowed by another guy.

I already told you I had a bit of a dilemma around this whole thing at the start of my adventures in San Francisco. I just didn't mention how it turned out. Not directly anyway, and I debated whether to come right out and say it because it really shouldn't matter—you're trying to make each other feel good, the particulars as to how you accomplish that really shouldn't matter. But people get curious.[20]

In my case, there was a window where I was open to the idea and then the window closed. And while it's true my first full-on sexual experience left me feeling a little forlorn when the guy walked out the door right afterwards, it wasn't because of the position I'd been in. That had felt right and given me enough confidence to be able to tell the guy I was interviewing with at the agency I was a top. I started to live up to my billing and then, once I'd slept with Nick, there was little chance of turning back.

---

[20] I could just as easily ask my straight friends if they were on top or bottom the night before, but why would I want to do that?

I suppose it's a little ironic that the guy who solidified my position as a top is also the one I would have been most likely to roll over for if it had ever come to that. Out of fairness more than serious interest. It just never went that way. And then by the time I did get a couple offers a number of years later it was no longer a boundary I was willing to cross. I'd already had a finger in my ass by that point, and not being all that thrilled with the feeling, it was hard to imagine that bigger would be better (still love ass play, though, if you're thinking about taking me to dinner).

You could write a whole book on this top/bottom thing. I'm not the one to do it, though. Hopefully, there's some versatile guy out there who can take up the cause, explaining what it's like from both perspectives, and removing more of the stigma. When I first heard about versatile guys who wrestled it out to see who topped, I remember liking the idea theoretically. Thinking that would make a lot of sense if you'd be equally happy with either outcome.

Along these lines, let me confuse you and tell you about another guy who I told, point blank, that he could fuck me, after I'd picked him up at a club in London and taken him back to my hotel. He was piss drunk and we'd been going at it for what seemed like forever when, at a certain point, he started talking all cocky, ragging on about how he'd soon be the one fucking me. He'd barely had a hard-on the whole time, and I was like, *Buddy, you'll be lucky to make the twelve steps to the bathroom without hitting a wall.*

When he got back, I was lying on my stomach and told him to go for it. Knowing that he weighed less than me, that I would've flipped him if it came to that, but also knowing it wasn't going to come to that (sure enough he came back to the bed, mumbled something about "later," and passed out). Why was I egging him on? I don't know, exactly, my thinking here wasn't particularly sound and I'm sure you can see this wasn't really about sex anymore. It was about calling another guy's bluff when you're confident he doesn't have the cards.

And it got even more messed up because after he'd taken a cab home, I realized he'd left his belt behind and ended up taking it back to the States with me. It was a nice belt that fit, sure, handy to hitch up my pants with, but it was undeniably strange how I kept using it every single day when I was back working in the forest. How when I'd worn out the notch hole where I buckled it, I cut another one in with my knife so I could keep wearing it. I was holding onto the belt as a reminder of what, exactly? How much of a stud I was? How I was a real man? If anything, it was me showing my lady side, how it meant something for me to keep my virtue intact. A reminder that if I found myself with a similar offer again, and if I did ever have a wild hare and decide to go for it, I didn't want to just be spreading 'em unless I respected the guy I was with.[21]

---

[21] I realize there's some dissonance between this comment and previous ones suggesting a kind of interchangeability between tops and bottoms, and or at least a lack of judgment around position. Some of that can be explained by pointing out that this all happened before I'd gotten a full grip on my feelings surrounding the subject. But not all of it. Obviously, if every guy took this more conservative approach with themselves, I wouldn't have been getting laid very much, since I myself was hardly a candidate for such respect and even if I had been, wouldn't have been able to convey it in the opening five minutes. But I think there's a way you can consider something to be true and still recognize you're not cut out for it without also believing you're somehow above it. It was hard enough to imagine letting someone into my mind or my heart, and—physics of it aside—I just think it would've been a bridge too far letting someone into my body.

That brings us to the fourth and final exception I'm going to mention—Hockey Guy—a man I was serious about from the day we met. Fortunately, he didn't have any rules, or at least not the same ones I did, and I was all too eager to suspend mine in order to continue to see him. Most of them, anyway. Every time I caught him looking at me like he was on the verge of saying something, *Is there more to you? Should I expect more from you?* I just turned away, thinking, *Don't ask.* But I kept turning back for more.

I probably could've married this guy if I'd been the marrying kind but looking back, I have no regrets because—as my dad always used to tell me, *timing is everything, my boy*—and it wasn't the right time. Still, that didn't stop me from playing the little game where I looked ahead and guessed at what would end us. My own challenges should be crystal clear by this point, but the best I could come up with on his end was that he had a cat and he snored like mad, an almost charming habit that inevitably became a menace by 2 a.m. This is just another way of saying there really wasn't anything to gripe about, and even though we weren't boyfriends, I did for a second time consider the possibility of what it might be like to spend my life with a guy.

It's true I wasn't quite in love with him. But I loved him in that sturdy kind of way that certain marriages can be well built on and probably would've gotten there eventually. From what I've seen, successful love follows two different paths that land it in roughly the same place. You can love someone and then, after many years, that constant feeling can accumulate into something greater so that—if you're lucky—you wake up one morning and realize that somewhere along the way you did manage to fall in love. Surprise. Or you can start off head in the clouds in love, and then slowly, over time, bring it down to earth, infusing all those fluttering feelings with weightier factors like the reliability and trust you're going to need for the long haul. Again, if you're lucky. The first way generally gets knocked for not being romantic enough, and the second for not being grounded enough, but assuming they end up in more or less the same place, I wouldn't get too hung up on the order of operations. I think the older you get, the more you appreciate the benefits of the first path—the more you have the patience for it—and as this guy was older, he had quite a bit of patience.

His profile would've said something straightforward like he: worked in a bank, lived in Park Slope, played hockey. Since he was modest, it wouldn't have mentioned the most obvious thing about him, which was what a good guy he was. What kind of good? The kind that had him helping raise his brother's kids when his brother died young, leaving a family behind. The kind of good that meant one of his closest friends was among the passengers who rushed the terrorists on the 9/11 plane that missed the Pentagon. The kind of good that was too good for me at the time.

Here's a scene to give you a sense of where I was.

Some friends of a friend were opening up a new club deep in Williamsburg (because there weren't enough already). They were having some kind of afternoon soft opening before the big nighttime action, and when we got there, we were quick to mix in with the few smallish groups hanging around. The new owners had some weed, and even though pot's not my thing, and even though I was going to see Hockey Guy later that night and had never been anything but sober when I met up with him,

I figured I had plenty of time to deal with the minor effects and decided to take a couple of hits just to be social. It was a great space, the owners seemed like nice people, and it was like, cheers, here's to you and your future success.

Anyway, the stuff knocked me on my ass. And at a certain point I checked the time and realized the whole afternoon had disappeared and it was getting dark. I'd never once stood this guy up before or even considered it, so there I was running through the seemingly endless maze of an unfamiliar subway station trying to figure out how to get to Park Slope on time. The station was under major construction, and with the voice booming over the PA explaining these would be the last trains for the night before they switched to bus service, I realized that all the posters I'd seen plastered everywhere earlier would have told me what was happening if only I'd bothered to look. So I got down to the trains, both of them pulling up at almost the exact same time from opposite directions. And glancing around frantically, I had no idea which one was the right one. All I knew was that the wrong one would be completely wrong.

There was this busker in the middle of the platform, not doing anything but sitting beside his open instrument case, and as the doors opened on the first train—then the second—I caught his eyes. I stared at him with all the pleading I could muster, feeling like some religious fanatic who's sure the busker has all the answers and I've just gotta convince him to give them to me. And damn if he didn't look calmly into my eyes, bring his finger to his own eye, and then point it at one of the trains. The right one, as it turned out. Yeah, yeah, I know he had a 50/50 chance, I know he could've been itching his nose or pointing at a rat on the tracks or whatever but hey, no one's gonna convince me it was anything other than divine intervention.

Inevitably, that drug-fueled run across Brooklyn felt more dramatic than it actually was, so that by the time I'd arrived at Hockey Guy's door—late—I'd half convinced myself he would tell me to keep moving. So when I rang the buzzer and the door opened, I confessed like some knucklehead teenager out past curfew that I was kinda out of it and had lost track of time and was really sorry. I could feel the shame in my eyes looking at him, but all he did was shake his head and say something just right like, "Don't worry about it, get in here."

There are a couple points to be made about all of this.

First of all, when you're at the nadir of your life, as I surely was during this period, if you have something good happening when everything else is going to shit, protect it. Protect it like it's the last thing between you and certain doom because it just might be. I remember turning down potential meet ups with Hockey Guy when I was in a funk and didn't think I'd be capable of being a decent human with him. Nothing to brag about, but better than telling him I was going to be somewhere and then showing up half-ass or not showing up at all. Because once you flake, it's too easy to do it again, and then before you know it no one's taking your calls anymore. I can't say Hockey Guy kept me from running off the rails, because I was mostly off them the whole time we were seeing each other, but I generally had it together when I was with him, and that counted for something.

What else is unusual is you can see the kind of reverence I held this guy in. It wasn't a feeling I would've guessed I was even capable of, let alone one I'd enjoy having. But he brought it out in me, and this made him completely different from any other guy I'd ever spent time with, gay or straight. Look, my straight friends and I respect each other, we're impressed with each other on a regular basis, we compete—too much, sometimes—but it's not like we ever want to be one another. The idea is to learn from one another and then take the information to make ourselves more formidable. We look at one another more than we look up to one another. And it's not like I wanted to be this guy, and it's not like I put him so high up that he was on a pedestal (step stool, maybe), but I did look up to him.

I can't fully explain how satisfying it was to be able to do this, but if you've followed me this far, you can be sure I'm going to give it a try. It'd been a while now since I'd fully stepped into my role as the wrap-my-arms-around-and-hold-you guy, the tell-you-it-was-gonna-be-all-right guy (even when I was the cause of your not being all right). The hugger, the holder, the patter of hair, that had become me. And I kept it up even after I'd started going cold on the general populace because there were still those close to me that could've used some consoling and there seemed to be fewer and fewer people around to be able to give it.

I had not only come to accept being that person, I'd felt a certain amount of satisfaction in it, convinced I had some genuine comfort to offer. But my impressions of myself were so riddled with holes by that point I was having a hard time believing myself anymore. Maybe everything wasn't going to be all right and for one time—one lousy time—I wanted someone I believed in to grab hold of me and tell me that it was. I doubt Hockey Guy understood this about me—it wasn't the kind of thing I would've mentioned to him—but I allowed myself to lean into him heavier than anyone else I'd slept with before, and if there was ever a relationship that quieted the longing I'd felt in that dream back in high school, this was it. Holding him, being held by him, I did sense something inside me was getting settled, although I hesitate to say what.

Hockey guy and I never fucked. Not that the possibility was ever ruled out, either implicitly or explicitly, but it just didn't seem . . . necessary. The technical term for what we did do is frottage, but I don't like the technical term (what am I supposed to say, "We frotted"? someone work on this please). When we weren't in bed, I remember being in my boxers a lot, having pizza, drinking beer, watching sports, talking politics. It was like being straight but better.

STR8 ACTING, MASC, MANLY MEN

When a man expressing traditionally masculine behaviors pops up in the gay community, he is often referred to as "straight acting," a description that misses both ways. If you've got another guy's dick in your mouth, then you've gotta be doing one hell of an acting job to convince someone you're "straight," and yet if you feel comfortable in your own skin, then the idea that you're "acting" seems equally bogus. Referring to men who are neither straight nor acting as "straight acting" men just can't be right, although I'm going to continue to use it. For illustrative purpose. Lodging a minor protest by always putting it in quotes.

Calling someone masculine comes with its own set of problems. Not the least of which is that the word is currently in the midst of getting a makeover and remains something of a moving target. But until it's able to be pinned down better, I'm going to give myself a pass and continue to use this one too. In the old school sense. Feeling vaguely entitled to ditch the quotes because I am—by birth year at least—old school, and there's gotta be some benefits that go along with that besides impending AARP discounts.

Masculine behaviors often have nothing to do with a person's sexuality, of course. Most everyone has had the experience of meeting someone they think is straight or gay based on their mannerisms and then finding out otherwise. I know I had to get it wrong a number of times before I finally realized it was best to stop guessing. But it's difficult to resist the temptation because there can still be some overlap between the two.

I'll cop to the fact that very early on, when people would approach me at gay venues and ask if I was straight, I'd take it as a compliment. I shouldn't have, obviously, but I got over it pretty quick. First off, you can be sure that some of that perception of me was relative—as perceptions of all men are, depending on what type of pond they happen to be swimming in—and it's possible the background was causing some of my more masculine features to pop. On the other hand, this was happening at *gay venues.* Like, yeah, there's an outside chance I really am a straight guy here with my gay buddy trying to show how supportive I am, but come on, what's the likelihood of that? I began to suspect that for at least some of the question askers it was just an opening line, but I couldn't get used to it, and considered it an awkward start to any conversation.

At least people were being friendly, though; because while it's true that "straight acting" men can often be sought after in the gay community, it's also true they can be looked down upon (sometimes even by the same person). If you happen to be perceived as masculine, and it's known that you're up for messing around with other guys, there are those who will accuse you of expressing some kind of internalized homophobia. I don't think it's as big a problem as googling the phrase "the problem with straight acting men" makes it out to be—and prejudice against effeminate men in the gay community (and in all communities, in general) is certainly far greater. But you don't have to look any further than 2020 presidential candidate Pete Buttigieg—accused of being not gay enough, or not the right kind of gay—to realize it's out there.[22]

The thinking goes that any expression of traditional masculinity by a man who sleeps with other men is the result of some kind of self-loathing. You can't handle your attractions—ones which traditionally fall to a woman because a woman is the one who's supposed to be interested in a guy—so you compensate for it. By rooting out every last vestige of feminine behavior in yourself. Granted, this would be sad if it were always the case, but seeing as pretty much every man—gay, straight, and in between—has at least some internalized homophobia, then I'm not sure the concept is going to pull any extra weight with someone being "straight acting." It's not like, "You're straight-acting, you must have internalized homophobia"; it's more like, "You're a man living on planet earth, you must have internalized homophobia."

Unsurprisingly, I'm not one of these people who believe masculine behaviors are necessarily toxic. Most, if not all of them, have the potential to be useful to society and it's more a question whether they're being expressed at the right place at the right time (good luck figuring out exactly when that is, but you can try). Easier to point out are instances when masculinity goes

[22] https://www.businessinsider.com/mayor-pete-problem-column-backlash-new-republic-2019-7 The New Republic article making the accusations has since been taken down.

wrong—overdone to the point where it becomes a caricature of itself, obscuring rather than helping to define the person underneath—or very wrong—when its presence (or absence) is confused with the quality of someone's character, someone's gender, or when expressing it becomes an obligation, something you're required to display by dint of having a y chromosome. But the pressure to do just that is not likely to disappear overnight as guys are particularly susceptible to other guys' opinions.

Most guys, to the extent they've been able, will be whatever their peer group—and, if they're around, older brothers and the other men in their life—tell them they should be. Like, I haven't read about a mass teen rebellion in Papua New Guinea/Samoa where the boys are supposed to regularly ingest the semen of their elders as some sort of fertility ritual.[23] They go along with it. Just like boys here will go along with any American idea of what masculinity is supposed to mean, no matter how unhealthy or ridiculous. If you're told you'll never be a real man if you continue to "throw like a girl" instead of however you want to throw a ball, you're going to be inclined to change your pitch. A wise move, perhaps, if you're pursuing a baseball career, but otherwise you risk buying into a very shallow idea of what it means to be a man while simultaneously taking in the idea that girls are inferior, and already we're in a lot of trouble.

It's been a while now that I've felt comfortable being a mix of what I consider to be masculine and feminine features—the exact ratios of which I wouldn't even hazard a guess at; they change—and I find myself equally at ease whether I'm cutting down a tree or admiring the wildflowers that have grown

[23] https://en.wikipedia.org/wiki/Etoro_people

up around it.[24] The ability to run a chainsaw is, like many masculine traits, a learned skill, but then so is the ability to express your feelings properly, and I'm not sure if learning a lesson well makes it any less a part of you than something you were supposedly born with.

That's not to say there's never any acting involved. Whether it's when you first start putting your identity together or responding to some current situation in a way you think you should. But most examples of this strike me as innocuous. Exaggerating your dismay at being dragged to the opera by your wife, say, because it makes for better banter. Life requires (or at least appreciates) a certain amount of this, and it's less a question of whether you're taking on a part than whether you're able to enjoy the role.

There was a guy I was close with who was a mentor of mine in terms of racial relations. And when I say mentor, I mean he gave me the privilege of being in the room when he and a friend of his would talk for hours about how truly screwed up things were for Black men in America, and I sat there with my ears open and mouth shut, realizing that for a person who had considered himself somewhat enlightened on the subject, I didn't know diddly. One of the things I learned about this guy was how much he'd had to repress himself growing up, with his family, in his neighborhood, at his church, and when he showed me a video of him speaking on some TV forum a number of years previous—all deep voiced, long faced, no joy,

---

[24] I was recently searching online for a Monday-start calendar and found this otherwise perfect one covered in pastel blossoms. Did I hesitate? Yes. In part, because I do prefer plain stuff, but for the rest of it I gave myself a poke in the ribs and went ahead and placed the order.

classic CNN type panelist—I barely recognized him. Trying to act straight had been a daily chore for him, and it was only when he finally cut loose, got a little lighter on his feet, let his voice sing, that he became not the "gay acting" man, but the beautiful man that I met.

Contrast him with Hockey Guy or The Scottish Wonder. Or my former boyfriend, for that matter. Nick, remember, actually was an actor, but when he wasn't acting, he seemed so utterly and consistently himself and that self just didn't come across as stereotypically gay. Did he deserve a finger wagging because when he wasn't attached at the hip with me, out roaming around on his own, no one would likely have guessed he was actually part of a same-sex couple?

When I was with Nick, we were affectionate with each other in public spaces. At his best friend's straight wedding, we seemed to be doing all the things any other couple there might have done (including getting into a pretty ugly fight). Were we letting down the tribe by, what, not sashaying around enough during the reception (I think we danced). Or is it more likely that a few members of the tribe—members who should know better than anyone how important it is to feel like you're being yourself—would be letting us down if they were to make judgments about the type of same-sex couple we were.[25]

---

[25] You don't want to see me try to sashay, not only because it would be incredibly awkward (although of course it would be that), but because you shouldn't want to take any pleasure in watching someone do something they're not comfortable doing. This doesn't mean I won't be giving you a standing O while you're out there voguing. I love that shit. And I'm just as likely to admire a good move on the dance floor as I am watching a well-executed play on ESPN. But there are other sports I watch that I have little interest in playing, too.

Can you tell I'd like this matter put to rest? The principle seems so obvious: if people aren't being mean-spirited, then there's no need to be telling them how to act. Period. Unfortunately, the discussion doesn't get to end there for me, because there was a way I was letting the tribe down. And that's likely what gave a defensive edge to my criticisms above.

The way I saw it, the issue for me wasn't being "straight acting"; it was the tendency I had to limit myself to guys similar to myself when I was looking to hook up, a predilection you might have guessed I had from reading previous sections. You might also have suspected some of that had to do with my needing to fully settle into my own masculinity before taking on someone else's, and I'm here to tell you that you're right on both counts. But only up to a point. The point when I realized I was somewhat fucked up conducting myself that way, and then over the course of time tried to modify my behavior. Evolving on an issue necessarily means you have to start somewhere less appealing, however.

So for a while I was like, why in God's name would I want to get together with a guy who reminds me of a gal? Simply having a penis wasn't going to be any sort of deal maker with me—I've had one my whole life—so there had to be something else I was looking for. On one level, it made perfect sense because it's hard to imagine me getting bent in the first place if it wasn't masculine energy I was being attracted to and wanting to connect more intimately with. But on another, it made no sense at all. I was clearly interested in female energy as well, so why should it matter what kind of container it was bottled in? And seeing as so much of what I'd wanted to experience was about breaking barriers between me and other human beings,

I didn't like the idea that I still had some left standing. When barriers can't be taken down easily, however, sometimes the best thing you can do is chip away at them.

Escorting might not seem like an obvious way to accomplish that, but you can probably deduce that if you're an escort and you get all choosy about your clients, you're not gonna have too many of them. It's more about what they're into, not what you are, and there was obviously no masculinity threshold a client had to reach to book with me. Consequently, I saw a range of guys, and as simple exposure can do wonders for comfort levels, I had plenty of opportunities to get comfortable. But you've got to be open to what you're being exposed to for that to work.

I think of two guys I briefly worked with. Both by all accounts straight, and the first with a serious, long-time girlfriend. He enjoyed talking about her in what felt like a normal, natural way, but in conversation he'd also pop off a line like, "Sometimes when I'm sitting on top and grinding it out, it feels . . .you know . . .good." (To be fair, he also turned the slightest bit red when he said it, and then added something about liking the control being in that position, but that only made the comment seem more endearing.) His identity was basically solid, not up for grabs, and here he was making a connection with men in the gay community. "Hey, I can see the physical pleasure aspect here, we've got that in common." Whereas the other guy I'm thinking of talked derisively about gay people out of the side of his mouth, and you got the feeling that for all his experience, it had only been more grist for the mill. That there wasn't a single other redeeming feature in it for him besides the money.

For me, the net result of having had effeminate clients in the mix was unquestionably positive. I found the breakthrough point coming earlier when I could get past mannerisms and focus on how to best connect with the person standing in front of me. (*We both like figure skating, we can sleep together, what do you know?*) But it wasn't sufficient. I wanted a situation where I wasn't getting paid, where I took full responsibility for getting together with someone because I chose the situation, not because it chose me. Because otherwise there was a way I still could've said, "This is what I do for work and this is what I do for play," and left it at that.

It had been a while now that my brain hadn't been particularly proud of my dick's (and my profile's) preferences. Not like I ever wrote "No this" or "No that," but I can't pretend I didn't look for certain tip-offs, and even if it was more of a lurking prejudice, it was still around.

So one night I'd picked up on this guy's profile who seemed like a great catch for the evening in every respect. I liked his looks, I liked everything he'd written about himself. But at the very bottom of the profile he'd said something to the effect that—I can't remember exactly how he put it—he came across as girlish. This was not the spoiler you might've expected due to the fact that I was mostly occupied with thinking how remarkable this was. Guys don't usually trumpet their effeminate qualities, at least not so directly, and I was struck by the way he'd owned himself. I said to myself, you've got a real easy decision to make here: You know for a fact you'd hit him up without this comment, you know with this comment he only comes across as cooler. So hit him up.

I can't accuse the guy of false advertising. He looked just as he'd looked in his picture and acted much as he said he'd act; if anything, a little less froofie than I'd been expecting since I'd prepared myself for anything. Per usual, it was a bit jarring to encounter that much feminine energy in a male body, but he was remarkably consistent, and it threw me less than if some gesture or phrase had come out of nowhere. Above all else he was sweet—younger than me, so I automatically felt protective—and the more we talked, the more I realized how nice it would be to get naked with him.

There were a couple reasons I think it went well. The first being simply the slightest bit of effort I'd put into wanting it to. As with my approach with clients, I sure don't want to make it sound like I was doing him any favors. Coming down from on high to bestow whatever masculinity I had to offer upon this poor, limp-wristed, light in the loafers kid. I was just trying to be myself and let him be himself.

The second reason was that he was an incredibly good kisser. And I love kissing. It's the one thing many straight guys will tell you is just about the last thing they can picture themselves doing with another guy and the one thing any number of gay guys are willing to skip over to get to what they consider to be more important activities, but for me it's like this great equalizer—mouths are mouths—and when I first put mine to his, I felt like we were on the same playing field.

I would've thought that would have put the issue to bed between us, but when we went out to dinner together afterwards, damningly, I had a bit of a relapse. There he was with his hand on mine, lisping his way through his order, and I remember glaring at the waiter, thinking, *If you even look at him sideways, I am seriously gonna stand up and collar you.* The waiter wasn't the one with the problem, though. That would've been me—still—trying to not only work through a better idea about what it means to be a man but be willing to stand up for it in public. Over the course of the meal, though, I could feel myself loosening up all over again, and by the time we went outside to take a walk in the park together—the snow falling all around us—I put my arm around him, held him close, and felt fully proud to do it.

I think that night was so meaningful to me because—despite all the access I gave you to my inner thoughts and struggles—I really did spend the majority of it being comfortable rather than thinking about being comfortable. Both with him and with myself. It's my favorite example, it's not my only example, but I can't pretend there's a ton more. And I don't believe there needs to be.

First blush attraction has to come from something outside of us, and being that it's not fully under our control, it's not something we're going to change easily (if it's even possible to change at all). But what did start to change for me was realizing it wasn't that difficult to take a second pass at people. Not ruling them out automatically because of some preconceived notion of what I like, since what I really like is connecting with people. Particularly, genuine and interesting and decent ones, and I was costing myself the chance at a deeper connection with some of the very people I should have wanted that with the most.

QUICKIES

One thing that happens after you've sworn off long-term relationships is that you find yourself compensating a bit by finding intensity in the short-term ones. With strangers, in odd moments, because those are the ones you've made available. That intensity doesn't always have to translate to sex, however.

Early on in my travels, I was boarding a flight back to the ABQ and when the guy on the aisle noticed me slumping toward the middle seat, he stood up to let me in. His uniform underlined the fact that he was on leave from the military, and after we'd both belted in, we talked about that for a bit. Nothing too in depth, and nothing that led to the kind of endless chatter you can get on a plane where your seat-mate makes an opening comment and then you respond and then they respond and before you know it the conversation's run from takeoff to landing for the sole reason that neither person wants to be rude and be the first to opt out. Instead, it was staccato talk, where the next comment was about the beverage service, and then there was some back and forth on that, and then silence, and then twenty minutes later one of us wondered aloud about where we might be flying over.

Anyway, about midway through the flight, the guy let his leg rest against mine. Not all that out of the ordinary, I thought, with the airlines having lopped yet another two inches out of coach and physical contact with your neighbor being practically a requirement. But as he—ever so slightly—began to press his leg against mine, I reconsidered. It's still a straight world out there, so when something like this happens, you've got to check yourself like a hundred times to make sure you're not imagining anything. But even if it was a tentative move, it didn't seem to be an accidental one, and I decided to go with it. The connection above the tray tables was increasingly good, and it was like, yeah, why would we not want to mirror that down below. I was glad he'd done it and wondered if I'd ever have the balls to instigate something like that (as comfortable as I got with myself, I didn't become much of a public instigator). So I pressed back ever so slightly and then he pressed back more and while we continued to talk, the tension in that small space continued to build.[26]

When we were getting off the plane, the guy asked me if I could give him a ride, but I didn't have one to give—someone was meeting me—and I was mostly happy about it because there was a kind of perfection to the encounter the way it stood. Unfulfilled desire tends to stay with you longer, anyway, and I can still recall this episode with more clarity than dozens of others that have since blurred together.

In subsequent years, I'd have a number of —some would call them homoerotic—experiences, many not capped with something so seemingly deal-sealing as someone asking for a ride afterward. But I liked not knowing how far a connection might have gone with every person, or even being one hundred percent sure the other person was sensing the same thing I was. I just liked being open to it.

Someone had put together a massive party in one of the canyons outside of Los Angeles, and as I was visiting my sister at the time, I decided to go—along with three of the coolest cats out there, and I'm going to go ahead and mention their names, Debbie, Duran, and Diego, for no other clear purpose than

[26] Memo to uptight straight men: For Christ's sake, do not let this become a thing, where you're suddenly all paranoid that the next time some guy's resting their leg against yours it must mean they're trying to pick you up. Otherwise, there's going to be a lot of completely unnecessary fist fights back in coach, and it's already unpleasant enough back there. There are no coded rules here that I'm aware of—most interactions of this nature rely on a bunch of additional social cues—and this is just one story.

the three of them were like poetry together. There were a lot of happy pills floating around, and the vibe, from start to finish, was perfect.

There was a point, though, where I was so wowed by the music and the crowd that I knew—as I often do in such circumstances and with such feelings—that I needed to take a step back. Except there wasn't an obvious place to step back to unless I wanted to go rock climbing up one of the sheer cliffs that defined the canyon. After looking around for a bit, however, I noticed one area that was different: a series of rolling hills, one behind the next, leading halfway to the top of the canyon, before that last hill, too, ran into vertical rock. No one appeared to be up there so that's where I went.

Reaching the top, I turned around to survey the scene below me and it was like looking down from a cloud. All these miniature bodies moving around, the music muted but still plenty loud, and I took off my shirt and began to dance.

I did glance down again from time to time, feeling both a part of the crowd and separate from it, and for maybe half an hour nothing much else happened. But then I noticed one body moving significantly apart from the others and when I looked again, that same body had ascended the first of the hills coming up toward me. *Interesting*, I thought. And with nothing but positive feelings about this person, whoever they were, I watched them disappear and then reappear again over the top of each hill, completing the hike the rest of the way up to where I was dancing.

I'd realized it was a guy at a certain point, maybe a third of the way up, and he walked directly up to me looking entirely confident. Until the very last moment when he wavered, dropping his head, before picking it back up again and saying, "I'm not sure what I'm doing here but I saw you dancing and I was thinking I should come up and be by you."

Now I generally reserve the word "courage" to describe people who are fighting for their lives—in a war zone, in a hospital—but maybe you can appreciate as much as I did the bit of guts it took for him to make this journey without knowing what kind of reaction would be waiting for him at the end of it. I said something like, "I can't believe how cool you are for coming up here." But no words could've captured how truly cool I thought it was.

As to what prompted him to do it, who knows? It wasn't like I had a couch waiting so he could lie down while I whipped out a notebook and asked him questions. *So tell me, why do you think you're really here? Do you believe this is a drug related issue?* I doubt he could've even told me, anyway. What I do know is that he shortly took off his shirt and started dancing with me. And it wasn't like we were in the middle of some male bonding drum circle where you're expected to respect certain limits and keep a piece of yourself in reserve. And it wasn't like we were necessarily going to mess around, either, a possibility I felt rested more with me than with him. Even though it seemed like there was more than enough attraction bouncing back and forth between us, he'd been the one to come my way, and he just seemed so happy with himself that he'd made it that far that I found myself with little desire to push it. The right call, I think, because the clearer it became that we weren't going in that direction, the sexier it got.

Later, he'd invite me down to meet his friends in their tent, where it seemed from the bits and pieces I picked up that he was straight in his nine-to-five life, but up on that hill, I'd like to think we transcended all that. He'd let his guard down, and when we looked into one another's eyes, it felt about as good as any connection I've had with anyone.

DON'T LOOK

I saw this Netflix movie a while back that talked about how the amount of eye contact one guy can maintain with another is an indication of his sexuality.[27] Like if he's able to stare into another guy's eyes for more than 1.9 seconds or something pseudo-scientific like that then he's gotta be queer. Needless to say, I had a problem with it.

Problem being that looking another man in the eye has got to go back a long way. Caveman times, probably. Searching to see if Rokk or Kror[28] might be a danger to you, a rival, a potential ally. Does he seem honest? Can you trust him? Whatever the case, and with all due respect to the men of the Castro, there's just no way this belongs exclusively to the cruising community at large. When your best friend tells you he and his wife are about to have a kid, and you know how badly they've wanted that child, the near misses, the near despair, and here he is sharing the news with you for the first time and what you are you supposed to do? Look at the goddamn floor when you tell him, "Congratulations, I know what that means to you guys." If you look at him for more than 1.9 seconds does this suddenly

[27] https://en.wikipedia.org/wiki/4th_Man_Out

[28] https://www.fantasynamegenerators.com/cavemen-names.php
I think this was the caveman name generator I used (I mean, how many can there be?) but, in any case, I did get these online.

mean you want to fuck him to celebrate the impending birth? Gimme a break. So I don't like the idea of staring between men being co-opted for exclusive use by either gay or straight men. As I said, my guess is that since the dawn of time men have been looking into one another's eyes, and it's always meant something, and as to what it means, that's for those two men to figure out.

Having said all that, it was nothing but rough for a while as I tried to figure out what a stare with my straight friends meant once they knew I'd been sleeping with guys. Friends whose eyes I'd never had trouble looking in before, but now I was worried they'd think I was suddenly interested in dropping trou. And what the heck, like I've already explained, I want to be able to look in my friend's eyes when they're saying something important, which is generally everything (and nothing) when you're sitting on barstools. I swear, if you had the right kind of detection device you could've recorded the thoughts bouncing back and forth between us.

> Friend: *I hope you're not saying you want to fuck me with that look.*
> Me: *It's the same look I've always given you. Isn't it?*
> Friend: *Maybe. You don't think just because I'm looking back at you that I want to fuck you?*
> Me: *Of course not. Wait, you don't, do you?*
> Friend: [shrugs] *So I hear you've fucked a lot of guys. And you've never made a move on me. Sooooooo, if you're not looking at me like you want to fuck me that means . . . what . . . I'm not good enough for you?*

I could imagine all this and a bunch more besides and all

of it was speculation. All that bullshit distraction lurking in the background, having nothing to do with what we were talking about. For a while, I wished they never knew how my lifestyle had turned out, that we could just go back to the way things were. But you can't go back. You have to press through it.

As to what my friends figured out on their end, you'd have to ask them, but here's where I ended up. When I catch my close friends' eyes, in our more significant moments, I just try to convey all the love I have for them, which is so great that it knows few bounds, and I'm not going to be shy about putting that out there. In that stare, I try to include everything. Even the fact that yes, obviously, I would mess around with you if the circumstances were right (stuck on a deserted island?). The potential is there and I consider that potential not only something to be unashamed of, but an unqualified asset in our relationship. Know also that, for a long list of reasons, we almost certainly won't. Starting with the fact that it's just nice to spend time with someone you have strong feelings for and be able to look in their eyes without having to worry about whether you're gonna end up in the sack together.

TAXI CABS AND LESBIANS

It's hard to say when, exactly, an intimate stare becomes a sexual one, but if you're nervous about the distinction, I wouldn't recommend giving it to the guy standing next to you on the subway. Or the woman next to him, either. You've got to know what you're doing with it if you're going to have any hope of not getting them nervous, too, and what you're *doing* is not much of anything at all. The look is more the absence of a look—an attempt to convey openness to someone without preconceptions or an agenda—and it took me even longer to be able to master it with women.

Looking back, I'd say my progression in this area went something like this: Googly-eyes that I couldn't always control very well when I was a teenager, to really looking at a woman as I got a little older, confident when sex was on the menu, to wigging out because the sex was surely going to lead to the two of us picking out baby names together, to backing off completely and keeping my head down. I'd been in something of an arrested development and I needed to find some middle ground.

A pivotal night came in New York when a group of us were taking cabs between bars and I ended up sharing one with a woman. I knew something about her from a mutual friend, and more from the conversation we'd had at the bar, which could be summed up as: I'd been surprised she was single, she'd been surprised I slept with guys. It was a bitterly cold night, and when I shut the cab door and she snuggled up next to me, it felt like it was being done in a pally kind of way. But that feeling changed at some point going crosstown, even before she'd put her hand on the inside of my thigh.

My body appeared happy about what was happening, but my brain, as usual, was conflicted. I didn't think I was ready to have sex with women again, but I didn't want to be cold about it as some kind of preemptive defense. So having considered adjusting my legs to give her a little more room, I decided to take the opposite approach. The horse was already out of the barn, and I shifted her hand the slightest bit on top of it, smiled when I looked at her and said, "That's all I got available right now. Hope it's all right." It was so true, and I hoped she could see that in my eyes.

I can't say the look she returned to me was one of complete understanding, but she kept it friendly right up until the driver announced we'd arrived at our destination. Even if she didn't know what to make of me in the end, I didn't have any regrets. Sometimes, a mixed message is the purest one you can give.

As far as I was concerned, messages like that could've stayed mixed indefinitely. When the syllogism kicked in, it wasn't like I'd put an expiration date on it. Or even thought, *Let's do this for a year and then see where we're at.* No, the all-guy era was continuing in all its glory—it had been well more than a year, probably at least two—and I'd done a good job of convincing myself I wasn't really missing anything by way of the general female population. I couldn't help myself from flirting occasionally (although you would've been more likely to see me in action with the lady behind the counter at Duane Reade than at a bar), but mostly I'd been keeping a lid on it the weekend Bess came to town.

Bess was an old friend of Exception #1, visiting as friends tend to do when you have an apartment and sofa bed in the city. She was taking some time apart from her girlfriend, and her praises had already been sung well in advance of her arrival. When my friend asked about the three of us meeting up, I was like, great. I barely knew any lesbians at all—I knew how messed up that was—and yet it wasn't like I'd been able to put up an ad on Craigslist: "Lacking lesbian friends, please reach out soon."

It wasn't just that I liked Bess immediately, which I very much did; it was that having been told she was a lesbian—other than worry that some general douchery might come out of my mouth as a result of my L word ignorance—I felt I could otherwise relax, look into her eyes (for at least 2.4 seconds, anyway), be as charming as I pleased, and nothing would be on the line. I could have made a toast to it, this flirting without consequences, and I continued to celebrate right up until the moment it occurred to me that maybe it was unfortunate that there *weren't* going to be any consequences. And then further, that maybe there could be. Because by the third drink I'd let myself process the fact that she was flirting back, and that's when I was like, *I think I'd really like to get together with this person.*

Why with this woman and not the one in the cab? Well, I don't remember exactly how far these two evenings were spaced apart, but there's little question that the first experience made the second more likely. A case of warming up the engine. And although there was already an entry in my playbook for women I was attracted to (See also: Avoid Sex With), I'd never thought to put in anything specific regarding *lesbian* women I was attracted to. Which meant that even though my guard had been down with Taxi Gal (as being in a cab tends to preclude the possibility of any immediate follow-through unless you've got a really open-minded cab driver), with Bess it was completely down (she being a woman who wasn't supposed to have any interest in men sexually. . . for all time).

Now, given my own situation, it's hard to understand how I could've made this assumption, but seeing as I never made it again, allow me to pass on to the fact that when I first met Bess, I was probably feeling more *like* the woman in the cab; that is, extra comfortable leaning into someone who wasn't, initially, supposed to be available for extracurricular activities. And for all I know that's how Bess viewed me. Comfortable with, curious about. I have no idea what my friend told her about me, but it couldn't have been too bad with her agreeing to go back to my place.

When we walked in the door and flipped on the light, I realized I was still pretty messed up from drinking and whatever else we might have done that night, and that meant there'd be little chance of my being 100% in the hardness department. I'd long since learned that sex and anything beyond two drinks was a bad combo for me, so it was more nervousness about that than about having not been with a woman in a while that kept me on edge about how useful I'd be. As it turned out, I was able to make love with her, but it still felt like a bit of a flail on my end and I tried to console myself with the fact that 1) she seemed happy and 2) I would inevitably sober up at some point and have a chance to set the record straight.

That opportunity came just before sunrise. I was on fire, or so I thought, when she leaned up and whispered in my ear, "It was better before, could you take it easy with me." Wow, here was something to ponder. Had I really gotten in that much of a rut? All that pounding away with guys and now I was, what, turning into a one-trick pony? So we found a rhythm that seemed to suit both of us, and for the rest of the weekend, the thought was never too far from the back of my mind about how nice it was to be with a woman again.

Naturally, I broke all my rules with Bess. I think we had breakfast together that morning, and I continued to see her as much as she wanted to see me for the remainder of her visit. She was extremely self-aware, clearer than even I wanted her to be that she was in a transitional period and wasn't looking for anything to stick. And while in the not too distant future, Bess would go on to meet and marry a guy, I was satisfied with a mere rebalancing of the scales, whereby I was reminded I enjoyed being with a woman every bit as much as I did being with a man and that was good information to have going forward.

Is this the start of a new section where I reel off a bunch of encounters with women? Of course not. Weren't you paying attention earlier when I said I had a double standard? I never did like to kiss and tell, even back in high school when one of the few times I confided to a friend along these lines was when my girlfriend was really late and I was getting really panicked (you can see how well I learned from that experience). And besides, my sex scenes with guys have been pretty tame as far as these things go.

I do remember doing a back of the napkin calculation at the end of this run—straight to bi to gay to bi again—and trying to figure out whether I'd had sex with more men or women over the course of it. It seemed fitting that the results were roughly equal. In the sense that I'd had a similar amount of sex with a smaller number of gals as I'd had with a larger number of guys. Enough, in any case, to be able to talk about the differences between the two.

Let's start with lube.

Naw, just kidding, that's not gonna get us very far.

Why don't we begin by taking your average guy and your average gal and compare what it feels like to be with them using each of the five senses. There's not going to be too much surprise here—everyone's seen the average person walking down the street, that's what makes them average—and it doesn't require any great mental gymnastics to imagine what it might be like to be in bed with them. Just in case you don't want to do even the imagining work, I'll go ahead and do it for you, but there are risks you take by leaving me in charge. My impressions are, by nature, highly subjective.

Touch. You're dealing with the surface of two different planets here. Yes, a woman's skin is generally going to be smoother. So if smooth is a big deal one way or the other then you're going to notice. If you like them both, like I do, then this isn't going to be an issue.[29]

Taste. I feel like I should be saying a woman's mouth tastes sweeter but that doesn't really strike me as true. Most people taste like the last thing they ate, or smoked, or that piece of chewing gum they just spit out. Underneath that, yes, there's something but I'd be hard pressed to define it. I'd say about the same.

Down below? No contest. I prefer the taste of a woman to any taste I might get in a guy's crotch area, which isn't so much bad as take it or leave it.

Smell. Sex smells are among this world's best smells, but, occasionally, they can be the worst. People are like, a guy's ass, how can you deal with it? I'm like, haven't you ever smelled a woman's way past prime pussy? Or pussy with yeast infection? Bad smells happen. But generally, I love the smell of both men and women and both in the same way. There's clean, which is

[29] Again, this is with the average person. There are guys out there who shave everything, moisturize their skin like it's their job (it is their job) and in general are plenty smooth. A side by side test with a woman finds them pretty indistinguishable.

nice. There's ripe, which is better. And then there's overripe, which is something to be overcome.

That's not to say they're the same smells. In fact, they tend to be completely different right up until the point where they become the same again: pure sexy smells. I understand how much overlap there's supposed to be between taste and smell, so you'd think I'd give the nod to the woman here, too, but I don't. I mean, this is sex we're taking about. It's supposed to be natural, not logical. I love smelling a guy's crotch the way I love sticking my hand down my warmups after a long run and getting a good whiff of that. Tie goes to the runner.

Sound. I'm a sucker for an accent, but accents come in all genders, and so do sexy voices.

Sight. This should maybe be the most obvious difference, and yet it didn't register that way with me. First of all, there had to be some irony in the fact that it was only by giving myself the opportunity to really look at men's naked bodies that I was finally able to put to rest any lingering concerns I had that I should have been more overwhelmed by women's. Private parts can be sexy at times, but also kind of goofy. I can only assume that it was at the point in human history where nakedness itself became an issue that these parts became extra sexually charged, with the highest charge going to the parts that were most likely to be covered up.

You can have a theory and still feel like you're backward compared to everyone else, though. I had the sense that most guys, gay and straight, saw some body part and suddenly became aroused, whereas for me it was always a sexual situation that caused these otherwise difficult to take seriously body parts to become sexy. And then it was not only those parts that got charged, everything about the person I was about to get intimate with had the potential to fire up. Their eyes, their feet. An elbow. Getting naked felt good because it felt good to be naked with someone, not because I was all hot and bothered about seeing their body.

Leaving out the easy stuff, like watching porn or having my dick rubbed, what gets me hard? The anticipation of sex. Touching someone. Kissing. Eye contact. With this lineup (and I don't believe I've missed a single thing here), how could I be any other way than what I am?

THE THOUGHT EXPERIMENT

I think we've laid out enough pieces of the puzzle now that we could try putting them together with a little thought experiment. One that shows the kind of bisexual I am or was or was capable of being. The primary benefit of doing this would go to other bisexuals, who could delineate the ways they are and aren't like me. To everyone else, the benefit would be to recognize the existence of those other bisexuals who will inevitably be making these comparisons and contrasts and understand that you're only getting one slice of the pie here.

This is a thought experiment because it requires many things to be true which were, in fact, true, but not all true at the same time. I got to be versions of this person, but I never got to be this exact person. For the purposes of this experiment, I'll walk into a medium size party (somewhere between a chiller and a rager) and assume that I am:

1. single and equally open to a one-night stand or an LTR
2. in my prime
3. in a maximally social mood, having worked in the forest for at least a week

That I have:

4. chucked my playbook and all the rules contained in it: about second dates, exchanging phone numbers, sleepovers, etc.

That I will:

5. walk in alone
6. have no more than two drinks
7. magically know someone in every cluster of people well enough to be able to walk up and say hello, and only some of those someones will know my sexual history, while none of them will have been a part of it.

Finally, with respect to everyone at the party, we'll assume it's filled with a mix of people, couples, singles, of various sexualities, known and unknown, with various degrees of comfort around their sexuality, but in the case of those who are truly not comfortable, no one's carrying a gun.

I'll probably grab a drink first, then stand somewhere near the bar nursing it. Scanning around, I'll notice some random thing. A woman absentmindedly pulling up a shoulder strap that keeps falling down and then, finally, letting it stay down . . . how much happier she looks now that she's given up the battle . . .

a man with interesting facial hair who keeps running his hand through it every time it looks like he's trying to remember something important . . .the way he smiles when he remembers it. I won't be undressing anyone with my eyes, and I won't be thinking I'm a freak for not doing it. I'm good with the fact that checking out people is a minor affair for me, and I'm just not built for going more than half a step beyond what they're offering.

But I'll also be comfortable taking that half step—observing the blouse on that woman and how one nipple will press up against it if she turns a certain way, or the jeans on that guy that suggest a nice ass rather than outlining every curve and crevice—because I know I'll soon gravitate back toward their faces—the anatomy, by far, that I'm most attracted to.[30]

It will then occur to me that I'm being a bit anti-social, so I'll make my way over to the acquaintance I know in group A, say hi, and begin a conversation. As I work my way around the room, I'll be attracted to pretty much everyone whether I'm introduced to them or not, as long as no one's being a jackass.

It might take me a minute or two to adjust if a guy is acting out of the box feminine or a woman appears more masculine than I usually go for, but I'll know it's just a residual from a hang-up I had, and I won't beat myself up over it. The longer I stay engaged with the person, the more it will recede toward the nothingness where it belongs.

---

30 If everyone went to a party dressed the way I'm most easily attracted to—suggestive but not over the top revealing—I would be the last person to accept an invitation because it would be so damn boring. This is just one man's taste, and the best reason to walk into a party is to see not only your taste, but a bunch of other people's tastes being reflected back at you.

I'll also know the difference between polite talk and flirting, and flirting and more than flirting, how two people can teach each other through successive comments and gestures and eye contact the way they're connecting. And if it's a well-stocked party, then there's a decent chance there will be someone I'm extra attracted to.

That doesn't mean I'll leave with them. These days, I'd be more likely to stay at the party as I don't get out very much. But since it's a hypothetical gathering, I'm gonna guess that if I do go home with someone, the chances are twice as good that it will be with a man. And assuming we do sleep together, that I probably won't have a desire to do it again. I won't have completely figured out why this is the case but having already decided I don't need to understand every goddamned thing about myself, I'll chalk it up to some general theory like I seem to be more willing to swing and miss with a guy. And that I just like sharing the knowledge of what we're like when all the clothes and bluster have come off—just a couple of guys—and that makes things seem somehow more real moving forward, not necessarily more romantic.

With a woman, I'll generally be slower on the draw. More likely to ask for her number, or, better, ask her out for a nightcap or a coffee somewhere away from the party and get her number there. If she gives it to me, I'll definitely call, and if we do eventually sleep together, then there's a high probability I'll want to continue sleeping with her.

If instead of a man or a woman, I get an offer from a couple—one member typically representing the interest of both in the three-way—I will feel a little full of myself, but politely decline. Just the same way I would turn down a male couple or a female one and for the same reason. All the three ways I was involved with were at least good, but none spectacular. Not having anything to do with the couple I was with, per se, but the fact that there was always one person I was more attracted to than the other and whether I handled that by paying more attention to that person or less, neither one sat quite right with me.[31]

Speaking of *not* hooking up, you know what else would make me equally happy? Intimately connecting with a man or woman who's in a solid relationship. Where I'm in the kitchen talking with one half of the couple and the other half walks in, and the look the two of them exchange reads like they're good. And I get the sense they know I'm good. Not up to anything but enjoying a moment in time.

When the husband leaves the room, the wife and I will pick up the conversation where we left off, her not afraid to touch my arm from time to time to emphasize a point and me lighting up every time she does it. Or if it's the wife leaving the room, I will look into the husband's eyes with all the intimacy I can muster as he continues to explain what really bothered him that week at work. In both cases, a reminder of what's possible. How a line can not only be held, but how holding it can sometimes result in more intimacy, not less.

---

[31] I don't have any experience with twins and I'm kinda irritated about that. I feel like I should have an example for everything. But if I ever decide to put myself back in circulation and come across any in or near my age bracket, I'll be sure to let you know how it turns out.

PARIS LAST

The closest I came to a scenario like this in the non-hypothetical realm was, in fact, my very last adventure before I settled down and got all monogamous again (well technically, I got celibate before I got monogamous, but that would be a blank chapter). I was capping off one of the best weeks of my life, having just come back from a solo motorcycle trip through northern Spain and southern France. I'd had a couple of connections along the way, minor ones, but it'd been just the right amount of time, and I was looking forward to getting back to Paris.[32] A woman I knew there was celebrating a non-birthday and she'd asked everyone to come to her apartment who'd help "compose the tapestry" of her sixty-seven-year-old life (I was a more minor strand).

The hostess had done her own identity shifting. A long-time secretary for a college in the Bay Area, she'd used her retirement as an opportunity to cut loose not only of the job, but of a husband who had grown increasingly abusive during their long but unhappy marriage. She'd taken half the proceeds from the sale of their home (which had appreciated monstrously during San Francisco's housing boom), decided to travel more, and had friends across the globe.

Our friendship had not only stayed intact through all my various incarnations—with boyfriend, with girlfriend, with no one—but had become increasingly flirty. She had her own

[32] You didn't really think I could've been one and done with Paris, did you? I'd been back every year, usually coinciding with a winter sale out of JFK, and I had a regular apartment I stayed in in Montmartre if I wasn't staying with friends.

paramours, of course, but at this party I felt the sexiness of our history come flowing through across the generations between us, holding her tight when we hugged, in a way you can't necessarily imagine doing when you're younger because you're not available to the possibilities.

Who else was there? Two brothers, both of whom I'd slept with. Together, on the same bed, all of us touchy-feely but nothing that would upset the neighbors. And separately, where the sex had been mostly an expression of the depth of the friendship between us and circumstances (basically, being unattached on a given night and feeling like it would be a good thing to do). I'd spent the night with the younger one before starting my bike trip and seeing as he was involved with someone else at the time, it was nice just to be cuddled up next to him in the morning and know that was a good stopping point.

The brother you wouldn't likely have guessed was gay was the one who always had been. That would be Yoan, who you met earlier. And while his brother Gilles did eventually follow in his footsteps, he'd only covered half of them, regularly alternating guys between the women in his life. I didn't know if I'd ever have sex with either of them again, but I was grateful that no arrangement had ever prevented them from treating me like a third brother (Fraternité! Liberté!). It might have even cemented that feeling.

They had seen me at—and through—my worst. Their nickname for me in such darker periods —La Boue—sludge, mud—a play on my name that reminded me that they weren't blind to my behavior, even if they loved me enough not to stand in too tall judgment on it. There were few secrets between us, and I treasured looking into their eyes and knowing that.

Who wasn't there? A woman they'd introduced me to my first year in Paris. A former girlfriend of Gilles who I'd been more than a little taken with but had never been able to persuade I was worth taking seriously. Audrey wisely recognized my immaturity, and yet somehow had always managed to stay connected to me while also standing clear.[33] Even if her feeling toward me wasn't as strong as mine toward her, I was still disappointed she'd been unable to come at the last minute, and spent the early part of the evening sequestered between the two brothers brooding about that fact. It wasn't until they told me she'd been spending a lot of time with a new guy that I began to face the reality that if something serious were going to happen between us it probably would've already happened. I can't say I was overly distressed about it—part of me was happy to hear her life was finally moving forward—and as the drinks continued to pour, I got my sea legs and started to tour around the room.

Before long, I'd settled in with a woman from Switzerland and a guy from Greece. The woman wore this impossibly red dress that couldn't have been a millimeter shorter without being too short for my taste, and her being in it made it the single sexiest dress I'd ever seen in my life. Leading you to suspect she wasn't wearing any underwear but, no matter which way

---

[33] Traceable, perhaps, to a night from a number of years back when all of us had been on vacation together. I'd taken ten minutes between drinks to bang a guy against the back wall of the dimly lit club, managing to piss off everyone I was with, each for a different reason. It wasn't typical behavior for me, but I'd had my reasons, too. She was the only one I would have explained them to—the only one who'd been surprised by my actions—but when she said, "I just don't understand you," the best I could come up with was, "Yeah, well, I don't understand why you won't cut loose from that boyfriend," and left it at that.

she shifted her legs, never letting you know for sure. The guy had a full beard and a voice that was both melodic and deep, surprisingly deep for how slender he was. And they were both my favorite kind of smart, not show-offy but quietly perceptive. I felt equally connected to both of them in that way that had me leaning forward on the edge of my seat the whole time whether I was talking or listening.

The conversation was wide-ranging, and over the course of it, I mentioned both my past boyfriend and past girlfriends in the context of whatever stories I was telling. It happened so naturally, sharing this simple information about who I was, and I wondered if it could always be this easy. I didn't know the relationship status of either of them beyond that the woman had recently separated from her husband, but I believed there was a distinct possibility they were interested in each other. If so, I figured my checkered past would give them a reason to get on with it sooner rather than later, but I'd continue to enjoy myself in the meantime. My cards were on the table, and I finally sat back in my chair to see how the rest of the night would play out.

The fact that I ended up getting together with both of them (the second after the first had left the country) shouldn't have made front page news. I can't say I was in top form with either one of them as there was no chance I was teetotaling on that trip. But it felt even better, in a way, not to feel like I had to impress anyone. It'd been nearly two years since I'd had any clients, and I felt like myself, not like someone turning in a performance.

What struck me more than anything else about that party, though, was the number of people in attendance who I could have imagined having a good life with. How I was aware from the first conversation with someone I knew well, to the last with someone I'd just met, that there might be ways we didn't match up, but they didn't seem nearly as important as the ways in which we did. And flashing back through my history, I saw all the people I could've had successful relationships with if only I'd been ready. Maybe I was ready now.

III. REFERENCES

"When Brandon was in his early 20s and studying abroad, he went on a trip to Israel with his friends to hike in the Judean caves. At a certain point, they reached a part of the cave that was pitch-black. 'It didn't take long for someone to suggest we all jerk off in the darkness,' Brandon, now 35, says. 'And so we did.' After they finished, they zipped themselves up and proceeded to continue meandering through the caves, as if nothing happened. They never spoke of it again. Brandon self-identifies as straight."[34]

— EJ Dickson, GQ, "Why Straight Men Are Joining Masturbation Clubs"

"We were both insufferably childish and high-spirited that afternoon and the spectacle we presented, two grown men jostling each other on the wide sidewalk and aiming the cherry pits, as though they were spitballs, into each other's faces, must have been outrageous. And I realized that such childishness was fantastic at my age and the happiness out of which it sprang yet more so; for that moment I really loved Giovanni, who had never seemed more beautiful than he was that afternoon."[35]

— James Baldwin, Giovanni's Room

---

[34] https://www.gq.com/story/why-straight-men-are-joining-masturbation-clubs

[35] Goodreads, Giovanni's Room Quotes

"The top two answers for what makes a person gay were 'kissing another guy' and 'becoming emotionally involved with a male sex partner.' So according to these responders, touching a cock isn't gay; lips touching lips is gay; and for that matter, heart touching heart is really gay."[36]

— Kyle Mustain, Slate, "Helping a Brother Out"

"A growing amount of heterosexual men are kissing each other on the lips and cheeks in order to bond, demonstrate friendship, and generally feel good, rather than for romantic and sexual reasons."[37]

—Lauren Vinopal, Fatherly.com, "Why Straight Men Are Kissing Each Other"

"Colton Haynes, 32, an openly gay actor from Teen Wolf, took to TikTok in March to call out the homiesexual trend. 'To all the straight guys out there who keep posting those, "Is kissing the bros gay" videos, and laughing, and making a joke of it: being gay isn't a joke,' he said."[38]

—Alex Hawgood, New York Times, "Everyone is Gay on TikTok"

---

[36] https://slate.com/human-interest/2018/12/bateworld-straight-gay-masturbation-meaning.html

[37] https://www.fatherly.com/health-science/why-straight-men-are-kissing-each-other/

[38] https://www.nytimes.com/2020/10/24/style/tiktok-gay-homiesexuals.html

"So I had sex with a woman on the ship. And I went through this whole thing, you know, I was like, Am I gay? Am I straight? And I realized...I'm just slutty. Where's my parade?"[39]

— Margaret Cho, I'm The One That I Want

[39] https://www.youtube.com/watch?v=YhdNnsgZFHU

THE STRAIGHTS, THE GAYS AND THE BI S

It's gotten harder to be a straight man in America, and you don't have to look any further than your bathroom cabinet to see it. I remember stepping back one day to really marvel at the sheer number of grooming products our boys had accumulated (many of which I, myself, now own) compared to what I had at their age (basically deodorant and a comb, both used occasionally) and thought how much expectations had changed. If I had to pick a single tipping point, it might be the day back in the nineties when that billboard of a nearly naked Mark Wahlberg went up in large cities across the country. Men were now officially fair game in the hot-or-not department, and men of all ages have been dealing with the consequences ever since.

It's not like a guy's looks never mattered and it's not like they're all that matter now. But the shift is hard to miss. Just look to Hollywood, where there's always been pretty boys running around but until recently, they didn't necessarily run the box office. If you're into old movies like I am, then stars like Humphrey Bogart are going to come to mind. It just didn't seem like things had been set up in such a way that you were drawn to the idea of fucking Bogart. You wanted to be like Bogart. Who you wanted was Bacall.

Not like Bogart (or Wayne, or Quinn, or Eastwood, or Nicholson, or Hoffman, or Pacino, or De Niro) was ugly, but you didn't get the feeling they were cast for their looks. They had the kind of charisma you wished you could find in your underwear drawer; you certainly knew you weren't going to get it by applying a bunch of products to your head.

Of course, I imagine there must have been some 100% gay guys who did, in fact, want to fuck Bogart, the way I imagine 100% straight guys today have no desire to fuck whoever the latest beefcake happens to be gracing the cover of *GQ* or *Esquire* or *Men's Health.* But all guys are being groomed to recognize sexiness in other guys now, and if you've got even the slightest availability to being swayed by such claims, then you might feel vulnerable.

The far right would have us go back to the fifties and scrub these images from our sight. Have us be presented with only wholesome family fare that would bring out the real men in all of us. The question isn't whether it would have some effect. I think you have to concede it would. Input is going to equal output to some degree. The question is whether that would be a desirable effect.

If you get a chubby watching a same-sex scene in a mainstream movie—one you might never have known you were capable of getting because you wouldn't have previously had easy access to such a film—is it really worth banning the movie because of you and your little chubby? Are you worried that's Satan there in your pocket, or could it just be a natural response to a sex scene that doesn't merit a whole lot of additional analysis? If you're the guy's girlfriend and you reach across to grab his hand and accidentally discover what's happening, does this mean you should be up in arms about Hollywood's corruption of your boyfriend? Do you need to have a deep worry about whether your boyfriend's gay when the odds are so heavily stacked against it? [40]

As a modern straight man, you've got to walk a vanishingly thin line. On the one side of it, you're expected to be able to *see* that guy on the screen or up on that billboard is sexy (otherwise you're going to come across as repressed and consequently less straight), just so long as you don't *feel* that he's sexy (then it's time to break out the lavender sleeping mask).

Fortunately, there are a lot more opportunities today to dip your toes into same-sex interactions without feeling like you're turning in your straight bonafides. Bateworld is one, an online community where guys get off together or at least talk about getting off together within the privacy of their own homes. Maybe I'll do a little research project one of these days, but at the moment all I can do is report someone else's: According to one survey, fifty percent of Bateworld members identify as gay, thirty percent as bi, and ten percent as straight.[41] There are jack-off clubs where you can do the same thing in person. I went to one in New York, and while the group effort wasn't exactly my style, I'd say it was better than bowling. An annual survey of one such club currently in operation puts the number of

[40] Americans vastly overestimate the number of their fellow citizens who are gay compared to the number of people who actually self-identify as such. To the tune of four to five times greater. There are various theories to explain this gap, but the most obvious one to me is that people are picking up on potential sexual fluidity, and—unwilling or unable to process the complexity of what that means—are quick to file it under "closeted gay" and leave it at that. https://news.gallup.com/poll/259571/americans-greatly-overestimate-gay-population.aspx

[41] https://slate.com/human-interest/2018/12/bateworld-straight-gay-masturbation-meaning.html Another 4% of Bateworld members call themselves "solo-sexual" while 5% would "rather not say."

self-identified heterosexual participants, again, at ten percent.[42]

So what to make of these guys who consider themselves straight but aren't all the time? Well, I hooked up with a number of guys like this and we did actually talk sometimes; it's easier to spill your guts a little when you know you're not going to see one another again. The common refrain was that they'd only ever had girlfriends in the past and didn't want or expect to be having anything but girlfriends in the future. Like me, they were making clear they weren't into relationships, but more than that, they couldn't even seem to imagine having one with another man and viewed the messing around as an easy way to blow off steam while single.

Now, I suppose every last one of them could have been lying, but I like to think I have a decent bullshit detector and it's hard to understand what would have been gained by doing it. Mentioning wives or girlfriends is something guys will dangle in advance as a potential reason for meeting up (look how straight I otherwise am), but I generally avoided hitting up guys who thought "girlfriend out of town" was a selling point. If I was already there, though, what would be the point of bringing up girlfriends at all unless it was a real thing you wanted to mention.

What did give me pause, however, was the way the information seemed to have been suggested as evidence supporting the idea that not only weren't they gay, but they weren't bisexual either, as none of them would use the term to describe themselves. Seeing as the operative word contained within bisexual is, in fact, sex (it's not bi-relationship-al or whatever), I was like, *How can you get more bisexual than regularly sleeping with both men and women?*

---

42 https://www.gq.com/story/why-straight-men-are-joining-masturbation-clubs

But in the end, I couldn't really blame them. Despite the overall tenor of the last section (Look at all the interesting adventures I had and isn't it swell how comfortable I got to be with myself), it was never an easy label to wear. It still isn't. There are some unique challenges that go along with bisexuality, but it might be easier to understand them if we first take a look at the ones that gay people have been facing for the past couple thousand years.

In case you failed to notice, the treatment gay people have received from their fellow human beings has historically been nothing short of hideous and no one should suppose there aren't more than a few wounds still being licked or that no fresh ones are being made. Sure, being gay meant you had a choice. You could suppress the vast majority of your sexuality—day after day, month after month, year after year—or you could express it and risk everything. Your family, your job, your place of worship—all of it was on the line. And, even if you were lucky enough not to have all those supports ripped out from under you, you still had to contend with outright malice from strangers. Being spit at, looked down upon, beat up. Or worse.

Bisexuals had a choice, too, although their options were far less onerous. If you happened to know you liked both apples and oranges, for example, then the idea of only eating oranges for the rest of your life could seem quite palatable. Or, if you did choose to grab an apple on the side, you could do it knowing that almost no one would be any the wiser for it. I heard even less about bisexual people growing up than I did about gay people and it's not hard to understand why. With all the hatred being shown toward same-sex attraction, you could probably count all the bisexual people who were openly dating same-sex partners on one hand.

But even *having* self-awareness about their sexuality would have been something of a coup back then because with so little publicity, I'm willing to wager that most potentially bi people wouldn't have even been fully capable of thinking of themselves in those terms.[43] In an odd moment, you might have found yourself contemplating an apple, *hm, that looks pretty good*, but because your love for oranges was so genuine, it would've been easy to brush off. And, never having tried an apple—thinking of it as some kind of exotic fruit—you wouldn't have known you were missing out on anything. Making the possibility of any other preference a non-issue.

I imagine there were a number of gay people who, as they prayed night after night to change the unchangeable, wished they had this option—to have their same-sex feelings be latent rather than visceral. Any option, really, that would've allowed them to feel they weren't selling out their soul just to avoid the scorn of society. And I bet a lot of gay people who were trying to make a go of being out wished that bisexuals who *were* hip to their feelings would've been just as open about them. It probably would've made everyone's path easier a lot sooner.

Fortunately, there were enough people determined to remain true to themselves that things began to change. People who were willing to cut their losses, wipe the spit off their faces, get

---

[43] It's a bet I would likely win as the number of people in anonymous surveys (where you have every incentive to speak out if you're feeling undercounted) who mention not feeling exclusively heterosexual has gone up dramatically. So, you either have to believe that something in the human DNA code has changed in the last twenty years, or you need another explanation. https://www.newsweek.com/more-people-ever-identify-bisexual-986297

up bruised but not broken, and keep walking with their heads held as high as they could hold them. And they kept walking, and marching, and demanding that every bit of their humanity be seen and accepted just as much as their neighbor's. And in so doing, they helped take a ton of weight off their bisexual brothers and sisters, so that today more and more of them feel comfortable coming out of the woodwork. "Thank you" doesn't really begin to cover it.

And while I personally didn't wait around for these rights to materialize to go out and do what I wanted, I still had plenty to be grateful for. Simply being able to walk into a gay bar and not have to worry about it being raided by the police was a huge plus. And a certain amount of progress had to have been already made for me to be able to start escorting at an agency that took American Express (certainly better than standing on a street corner, leaned up against a lamppost and trying to look indifferent).

Having said all that, in some respects, in Western democracies at least, the tables have turned a bit. So much so that more than one bisexual person has said—I myself have thought—it would be easier to be gay. People understand gay now. Or at least have a clue about it. And even though I've meant it when I've thought about it, I want to be clear. It's a passing thought. I don't want to be anyone other than who I am. And I don't want to make a flippant comment about what it's like to be gay, since it's still far from easy in most places. (Try going on vacation with your same-sex partner to Bahrain, for example. Or try living there.)

What sucks about being bisexual? In my mind, nothing. But what sucks about being bisexual in the world as it's currently constructed? Too much.

LET ME COUNT THE WAYS

It all starts in the womb where it feels like bisexuals are already having a hard time fitting in. There is an argument to be made that your sexuality—gay or straight—has a genetic component, or, depending on who you talk to, a strong genetic component. So what the heck genes are in play that allow you to be bisexual? If you're born with an inclination toward, or at least no major impediments to, getting together with members of your own gender, why not just go all the way and be gay? It feels, sometimes, like being a little bit pregnant. Maybe one day scientists will come up with an explanation, but at the moment no one's talking about the quest for the bisexual gene.

And in a way, this sets the tone for your whole life. Not quite fitting in with the world the way you've been told it works. Think about it. If you do consider yourself 100% straight or gay, then your sexual identity is constantly being expressed and confirmed when you're out and about. You show up to events holding hands with a girlfriend or boyfriend, husband or wife, and you don't have to say a word beyond, "Hi everyone, I'd like y'all to meet X" (the person I'm sleeping with whose gender implicitly matches the gender of every single other person I've ever slept with). There's no daylight between the history you know to be true on the inside and what people are seeing on the outside. There's nothing to explain.

But if you're bisexual and show up with someone on your arm who's the same gender as yourself, people are going to assume you're gay, and if you show up with someone of the opposite gender, straight. I know, screw the police and all that, but if you're not gay or straight then there are a lot of social situations that make you feel like you're hiding something. Or at least, like you're not being fully seen.

And it's not as if there's ever a single point in the conversation where you can easily correct the record. "Hey, this is my partner, but, just so you know, I've also fucked guys." Like where does that fit in? I think that has a lot to do with the reason I haven't been so open about my history, because it ticks me off that I should have to say anything at all. And with the massive exception of writing this book, I'm not one who's typically comfortable jumping in with a bunch of unrequested information about my personal life.

There was once an otherwise enlightened sex columnist whose initial columns on the subject of bisexuality conveyed the idea that, to the extent bisexuals might exist, they should use their own water fountain. To the writer's credit, these columns evolved over time, but I sometimes wonder whether the original ones didn't contain a grain of truth.

The only time I have truly felt at ease in social settings when it came to this type of thing was when I had a small but tight group of bisexual friends in San Francisco. It wasn't like when we hung out, we talked very much about being bisexual. Most of us didn't even use the word. But the feelings around the concept were almost all positive, believing we were really onto something. In much of the rest of the country, however, declared bisexual people are still few and far between, and it can be an uphill battle to try to maintain a position that feels authentic. On your own, in your weakest moments, you can start to question yourself.

Despite my history, I'm not one to advocate for sleeping around, but I will say it took a fair bit of sleeping around with both men and women before I was able to put in a strong enough framework to deal with this. Early on, after a particularly satisfying roll in the hay with someone of the same sex, I was like, maybe I really am more gay. I hadn't considered myself straight for years, and here, at least, was an easily defined category I could put myself into. But I wanted it not to just feel right in the moment, but to keep feeling right over time. And when it didn't, it was like being back to square one.

Almost no one seems to doubt that straight and gay people exist, of course. But with bisexuals, the crowd of public opinion is often trying to negate one part of you or the other. You're either "Straight, Gay, or Lying" (as one infamous headline from a major U.S. newspaper put it [44]). Or you're confused. Or you're just experimenting and will grow out of it. Even people who do allow for bisexuality find it too easy to dismiss.

One of my favorite examples of the whole phenomenon of glossing over bisexuality comes from William Saleton, a crackerjack writer with a seemingly endless ability to find interesting topics and write well about them. A number of years back he published "Brokeback Mutton: Gay Sheep and Human Destiny," an article based on an experiment that tried to uncover the sexual proclivities of rams and the statistics that resulted from that experiment.[45] Specifically, "A bare majority of rams turn out to be heterosexual. One in five swings both ways [that would be 20 percent if you're keeping score at home]. About 15 percent are asexual, and 7 percent to 10 percent are gay."

---

[44] https://www.nytimes.com/2005/07/05/health/straight-gay-or-lying-bisexuality-revisited.html

[45] https://slate.com/technology/2007/02/gay-sheep-and-human-destiny.html

You would think there'd be an interesting discussion here about sexual variety in rams, but no. Even though the gay sheep make up the *smallest* non-heterosexual anomaly in this sample, there's not a single word about anything other than gay sheep. All of which is interesting and worthwhile, but what about showing the bisexual sheep a little love. Or the asexual ones for that matter.

It's not surprising in a way because, if you think about it, it was never gay people that should have made straight people uncomfortable (or vice versa) to begin with. They not only define one another, they don't exist without one another. Bisexuals can make both groups uncomfortable because they mess with people's sense of their identity. *If you're not this and you're not that, what, exactly, are you?*

Part of the reason for this has to do with the word bisexuality itself, which isn't particularly understandable or, in fact, accurate. It's not like you're ever actively *being* bisexual. Sexual feelings come one moment at a time, one person at a time, and you don't have to be bisexual to understand this. Just walk into any bar and try to pick up two of your favorite gendered people simultaneously. I mean, literally at the exact same moment, you can't do it. And even if you're able to talk back and forth between them and get them both to come home with you, you're going to reproduce the same phenomenon when you're all in the same bed together. Three-ways I've been involved in have sure felt a lot more like a constantly shifting series of two-ways than anything else.

Now, if that three-way happens to involve more than one gender, it's possible you might get the occasional kumbaya, we-are-all-one sensation, a mass of flesh with six legs, six arms, and a variety of other appendages all writhing together. But if this does happen, it underlines my point even further because a moment like that goes beyond being with any given man or woman and, instead, feels like being part of some larger, multi-gendered or un-gendered thing—one where you shouldn't be able to tell where one person ends and the other begins. And if you're not having that moment, then you're right back where we started. Having a series of alternating hetero and homosexual moments, and therefore only actively being hetero or homosexual in real time.

Of course, "bisexual" works theoretically as shorthand for a person who is sexually attracted to both men and women. Partners of bisexuals can have a hard time accepting even the theory, however, whether they are of the same gender or the opposite gender of the bisexual in question. They worry that even though you're with them, in bed or holding hands walking down the street, you simultaneously want to be with someone of the other gender. As if bisexuality somehow conferred upon you the ability to be in two places at once. They have to deal with this little voice in their head that says, *Maybe I'm not enough.*

Having reached a certain level of comfort with the situation, I now know the better, and truer, response to give to a partner with this insecurity. And that is to say, "You're being insecure about the wrong thing." It shouldn't be based on my sexuality. Rather, it should be based on my ability to be monogamous. If I'm not predisposed to being monogamous, then, no, you're not gonna be enough. And if I am, then you have nothing more to worry about with me than with any other human being involved in a monogamous relationship. I'm sure to notice people I'm attracted to like everyone else. Very occasionally, like everyone else, I'll be tempted. But presumably, because I like being a monogamist—accepting the drawbacks along with the benefits—I'm not going to do anything about that temptation besides maybe take the memory of it home with me at the end of the day and bring some extra spark to the relationship I actually signed up for.

I realize I've only got one experience to vouch for my same-sex monogamist credentials—meaning one boyfriend—but I feel like he was a pretty strong example because it wasn't just that I didn't cheat on him, it was that I never came close to doing it. I mean, I was working at a sex club during the back half of our relationship, where temptations didn't just come knocking at the door every night; they walked right through it. I feel like a bell or two would've gone off if this was going to be a problem.

For whatever reason, being in a monogamous relationship seems to cut way down on the number of people I'm sexually attracted to. I assume this non-willed feature is one of the main reasons why I can be in a monogamous relationship in the first place, as it's not for everyone. Statistics vary widely on the number of people who say they cheat (and that's without even trying to determine who's being honest about it) but we can safely say that there's a bunch who do and a bunch who don't. If you don't have this autofilter—and I know a number of upstanding citizens who don't—monogamy would seem to make a poor choice because you'd be constantly fighting against yourself and you're bound to lose the fight sooner or later.

What about the argument that partners of bisexuals have twice as many people to worry about in the straying department? Like, "Oh my gosh, he could be out there wanting to have sex with *anyone.*" I don't know what to say about this. I suppose there's a mathematical argument to be made, but mostly it strikes me as ridiculous. The bisexual people I've known, while, yes, being attracted to a large number of people—meaning happy in the company of, even the close company of a wide variety of people—are not actually into jumping in bed with all that many of them. But beyond the anecdotes, even if you could somehow rig a test of all the people on earth comparing the number of people a bisexual person would be tempted by with the number that a straight or gay person would be tempted by—who would really care what the exact numbers might be, since all it takes is *one* person to stray with.

Does this mean that none of the nightmare scenarios that people associate with bisexuals —always going back and forth, never able to make up their minds—exist? No, they can exist. On a variety of levels. Here's a fairly harmless example to illustrate one of them.

So I was en route to my favorite burrito shop in the East Village. Not like anyone can make a burrito in New York the way they do here in New Mexico without the chile being fresh, but I liked this place because they didn't try to imitate, just did their own thing with them. Anyway, this woman was walking by in the opposite direction, and she passed so close to me, smelling so damn good, a mix of her and her perfume, that I literally turned around and followed her for a few steps before I fully realized what I was doing. Once I'd gotten turned around again, I tried to figure out what the heck was up with me. And before long it came to me that I'd pretty much had it with guy stink. Like, done for the moment, and I did take some time off from my carousing in recognition of that fact.

Now, regardless of your orientation, allowing yourself to be shifty like this is one of the unquestionable benefits of being single. But this minor example points to a more major one, one I alluded to earlier when I talked about how nice it felt to break my dry spell with Bess. Because I'm sure the same thing would happen in reverse if I ended up being with a man again after having spent a long stretch of time with a woman. The question isn't about whether it would feel good, I'm sure that it would. It's rather, would that feeling point to some sort of fatal flaw in bisexuality itself, which I don't think it does.

Haven't you ever gotten back together with an old boyfriend or girlfriend and thought, hey, it's nice to be in their arms again, they were always so [fill in your favorite unique characteristic about the person here] and my last partner never offered that. Lacey enjoyed traveling but didn't think much of dogs, Linda had three of them, but she was a homebody. You like both, but you're not going to be able to take the dogs to Vancouver with either of these women. I mean, that's the entire essence of choosing a partner, right? That you're agreeing to get (and hopefully give) a lot of benefits, but there's no way you're going to get all of them. Or at least, it's going to be hard to get all of them.

I've saved the most intense level of this issue for last because, frankly, it's a bit out of my league. This is the one involving people who, in the very depths of their being, want to feel the touch of both a man and a woman regularly, consistently in their lives. I know of couples who've ended up in therapy for this, where one partner is dealing with these conflicting desires and the other is trying to deal with that partner, and the best I can do is throw out a few suggestions: Get single until your feelings resolve and stay single if they don't. Ask to open up the relationship in any of the myriad number of ways that can be done, while recognizing that getting permission to try something new might be the easiest part. Be honest, but remember *your* honesty will only get you so far, and if you want to keep the relationship, you're going to have to keep returning to your partner to see how they're coming along. Every situation's different (do you have kids or not?), every partner's different (some are more open than others), and whatever solutions you come to are going to have to be reached together. Both of you, hopefully, understanding that this is the advanced level course where you're not trying to establish if someone is "gay," but moving beyond that.

When I was sleeping with 100% guys, did that make me 100% gay? In practice, yes. In theory, no. My feelings for women didn't just disappear. I was monogamous with the same woman for eleven years. Did that make me 100% straight during that time? In practice, yes. In theory, no. I assume I'll always remain capable of responding sexually to both genders (as long as I'm capable of responding sexually to people, period), and what's happening at any given point in my life isn't going to change that.

I highly doubt when I'm out at a party and deciding about who I might like to go home with—deciding in a way that won't be genitalia based—that what's actually going on in the back of my mind is some kind of fiendish plot like, *Ha ha, I'm really gonna collapse the hetero-homosexual paradigm tonight.* But it kind of looks like this: Gay gay people (understandably) have a huge investment in it. Straight straight people (less understandably) have a huge investment in it. And bisexual people would rather not talk about it.[46] Because many of us have a hard time understanding what ultimately there is to talk about. People are attracted to people, it's like attraction 101, and it's only when you find yourself being squeezed by the two sides that you feel compelled to say something—like "Hold on a minute"—or write something—like this book.

Did I feel more gay than I have in a long time while I was writing this one? Absolutely. I immersed myself in gay memories, gay websites, gay news articles, gay movies. My dreams even changed.[47] And that got me to thinking about "conversion therapy" and how it might well have been started by some misguided bisexual.

To be clear, I think of conversion therapy as nothing less than a kind of torture for gay people. Yanking a fish out of the water it had been contentedly swimming in, throwing it on the pavement, and telling it to breathe. And then berating and berating it because it's not breathing.

I say I wouldn't be surprised if it was some bisexual person who came up with the idea, because having access to both sides of their sexuality, a bisexual would've been more likely to believe you could focus on only one. "I did it. So can you!" Does this mean there should be— not "conversion therapy," but, I don't know—single-minded-focus therapy for bisexual people. Uh, no. First off, maybe it's just me, but with the documentaries

[46] https://www.pewresearch.org/fact-tank/2019/06/18/bisexual-adults-are-far-less-likely-than-gay-men-and-lesbians-to-be-out-to-the-people-in-their-lives

[47] This example got messed up. Not like I have many overtly sexual dreams, but the two and a half ones I did have during the early writing process were distinctly gay and I was going to headline that. But then . . .

I've seen, a lot of the guys running these programs seem like the last sort of people you'd be able to take advice from with a straight face. More importantly, you don't need to register for a seminar to figure this stuff out on your own. If you're in a same-sex relationship and if for some reason it bothers you to be having dreams about opposite-sex partners, then consider cutting back on the straight porn. If you're in an opposite-sex relationship, you're probably not gonna want to be spending every other weekend dancing at Rainbows. And if you find yourself really wanting to, then that should tell you something.

During my salad days in San Francisco, I was out at a mixed club—mostly straight but still plenty of gay to go around—and when a guy I'd been introduced to asked me to partner up with him on the pool table, I said, "Sure." He was Type A masculine with a cowboy hat, and as he also turned out to be a ringer, we ended up staying on the table for quite a while. Over the course of the time we talked about this and that, I don't remember anything specific, but at a certain point he said he wanted to take a break, and as he was calling the shots, we took one, off to the side, with our drinks. That's where he asked me my take on the whole sexuality thing.

At the time, I only had a very rudimentary prototype of what I've written here available, but that's what I gave him. I said I thought there was a range, and then waited to hear his angle, assuming he had one. Looking me square in the eye, he told me, "I have dreams about guys all the time. And I'm never gonna do anything about it." He didn't seem sad when he said it, no trace of regret in his voice, but he didn't come across as angry or defiant, either. It felt like he was just stating the facts. And I believed him.

I didn't ask, but I did wonder if he came to a club like that to prove to himself he could stay removed from what was happening around him. Or if he came because he wanted to get close, but that was as close as he wanted to get. It's not like I hope he did anything to alter his stance—that was his business. But what I do hope, especially considering what a good guy he seemed like, is that he didn't drive himself crazy with it.

Is a guy like this gayer than one who dreams exclusively about women, but for the fun of it has a fling with another guy when he's backpacking around Portugal? What about guys who are ostensibly straight but mess around with other guys due to circumstances—prisoners, actors, gay for pay, or single and simply wanting to "blow off some steam"? There's a way they're obviously gayer than guys who've never done it—they've crossed that line, after all—but, if you think about it, there's a way they're straighter too. They've tried and they know they're not particularly interested. At least not longer term or under normal conditions. For a guy who's never tried, there could always be that suspicion in the back of his mind that he might like it. And he might.

What would a 100% straight person look like? I imagine such a person having the same reaction to someone of their own gender as I have to my brother-in-law. Great guy but nothing—at all—registers sexually. Except, unlike me, the extreme straight guy has this nothing-feeling toward every single living, breathing male on the planet. No thoughts about sleeping with guys, no dreams about sleeping with guys, obviously no actual sleeping with guys and no exceptions to that no matter what the circumstances. It's a bit of an ask, but I'm sure it's possible.

A 100% homosexual guy? I'd say someone with not only little sexual interest in women, but even active disinterest. The thought of being intimate with a woman makes them think, blah. The purest of this breed would never even have messed around with a woman at all, but to the extent they might have, the more intimate it's been, the more blah they've felt about it. In the most extreme cases, vagina would equal turn-off, and in the rest, not nearly enough of a turn on. These are often the same guys who will tell you they've known they were gay since very early on. Like way before someone like myself even had a thought about having sex with anyone. The same ones who will look at you cross-eyed when you talk about being gay being a choice and who can blame them.

Even here, though, you never know. I knew a guy in LA of this capital G variety who agreed to be a sperm donor for a woman, a very good friend of his and self-described lesbian. She asked if he'd be willing to do it the old-fashioned way, because she wanted it to be what she thought of as a more natural conception. He was not looking forward to this by any means, but said he'd do his best. Well, not only did she get pregnant, but lo and behold, right there in their early thirties, they decided they liked being together. In bed, too. I have no idea if they're still together, but the fact they even made it that far stuck with me.

Also, I'm reminded of something an older friend who was on the front lines of the gay revolution told me. He said, "You know the big secret back then was that being gay didn't mean you slept only with guys." I was like, doesn't that kinda make the guys who did that something other than gay?

Maybe it's just the company I keep, but I don't know a single person whose sexuality appears exactly the same as that of any other person I know, and it's hard to match that up with what much of society is still inclined to see as a black and white issue. Our youngest generation seems to grasp something of this discrepancy,[48] as they are much less likely to view themselves as exclusively homo or heterosexual, and I do hope that holds.[49] Because the closer you look, the more the divisions start to break down. And when you add in gender identity the whole thing really falls apart.

THE FINAL BLOW

It kind of astounds me that it took me so long to make this connection. Sure, I would read about people's behavior toward transgender or gender fluid or, more recently, nonbinary people, and think, *I wish people would stop being such dicks*. But I didn't feel *invested* in it. And I should have been. Not just as a fellow human, but as a fellow traveler trying to make their way through life astride two worlds.

---

48 https://news.gallup.com/poll/329708/lgbt-identification-rises-latest-estimate.aspx https://today.yougov.com/topics/lifestyle/articles-reports/2020/06/01/sexuality-spectrum-pride-lgbtq-poll

49 A forewarning to all you enlightened Gen-Z-ers out there: you might be surprised to learn how, as you get older, the culture has at least as good a chance of changing you as you do of changing the culture, and what you really should be shooting for is to get enough people on board that there's a kind of herd immunity developed against ignorance. Otherwise, the population can get re-infected, old ideas can come back with a vengeance, and if they spread, your gains will be lost.

Gender identity was kind of like the final frontier for me, and I'll admit to having to cover some distance to get there ("there" meaning reaching the place where I could even begin to appreciate the expanse of territory still spreading out in front of me). As a younger man, I didn't know what to make of gender-bending activities and consequently lumped them all into the shallowest category: people who, for whatever reason, wanted to appear as the opposite gender. But even on this most basic level, I couldn't get it right.

I was checking a guy in at the club one night and he asked me if he looked familiar. I looked closer and shook my head. *No, I didn't think so.* He smiled, and then completely changed his voice while cupping his hands over his chest. "You just don't recognize me without the tits!" I couldn't believe it. It was my favorite host at Trannyshack, the one who was always giving me a hard time about *my* mannerisms—basically boy-next-door and therefore boring—who gave me a hard time about everything, really, but with a big eye-lashed wink, and I busted out in a huge smile. I don't think it was just at the pleasure of being surprised. It was seeing what was under the makeup—a guy just like myself—and thinking that maybe I—for the first time—was just the littlest bit in on the joke.

I thought about it later, and realized I'd been little better than a tourist at Trannyshack. Easily accepting what I was being shown, like it had no relevance to me. Here were the first inklings that it did, but as the costumes and performances there tended to be highly exaggerated, it still struck me as a kind of game. Something surface which, like the makeup, could be washed off in the morning.

Enter Justin Bond. In New York, a number of years later. He may not remember me, but I had the privilege of hanging out with him on a number of occasions and won't ever forget how easy he was to talk to. How casually brilliant and talented. His main gig was a show called Kiki and Herb (he was Kiki) and the way he would utterly transform himself onstage was nothing short of spellbinding. This wasn't about wigs, or shiny, dangling earrings. Justin seemed to have full access to the (harsh but) feminine part of himself and he could transform into it as quickly as he could light a cigarette.[50] It was a whole new level for me to experience, how far below the skin he was able to go. But I was still a passive bystander witnessing it, and he was still either Kiki or Justin, distinctive-ish genders in time, even if occupying the same space.

I continued to enforce something of a wall between the genders for a number of years after that, the material making it up increasingly thin, but holding. But things finally came to a head a couple years back at church when we had a guest preacher come to town. While this person was setting up for the service, I checked them out—once, twice, three times—then turned to our daughter and asked if she thought it was a man or a woman.

The curiosity wasn't quite innocent—I sensed something unusual—and once the sermon began, I realized it didn't matter what had prompted the question because it had been a bad one. One I promised myself I would never ask again. It's hard to imagine how your kids will turn out any better than you if you're unable to keep some of your weaker instincts to yourself,

---

[50] Justin had a great line about Kiki and Herb losing the Tony for best variety show to a ventriloquist act, which he delivered after exhaling a huge puff of smoke. Pause ". . .I can't believe we lost to a fucking Muppet."

and as I listened to the preacher talk about what had led them to becoming the person they were today, I was wanting the service to end just so I could clear things up with our daughter as soon as possible. Once it did, I said to her, "I hope you can see I had no business asking that question," and proceeded to underline a number of the points the preacher had just made while continuing to reflect on the type of quality person we'd spent an hour with.

In part, to make amends for this, I began to seek out gender fluid documentaries, listen to gender fluid TED Talks, and, perhaps most importantly, I started going to our local CVS more. I'd rarely gone there in the past because the prices are so inexplicably high ($12 for a crappy toilet bowl cleaner, come on), but if I could think of anything to buy there, I tried to. I'd remembered there was a person working behind the counter who wore a mixture of facial hair and makeup, a person who I'd had a hard time processing in the past and, perhaps as a result of that difficulty showing in my face, had generally been coolish with me. But I made sure I got in this person's line every time.

Even if it was a little weird and stalk-y of me to do this, I felt like it was worth it just to arrive at the day where I had finished checking out, was about to bag up my stuff, and then couldn't get the plastic bag to open no matter how gently or roughly I tugged at the mouth of it. This was clearly a punishment for my using a plastic bag in the first place, but in any case, I wasn't sure I was even working the right end anymore by the time I glanced over my shoulder and noticed the line forming behind me. I pride myself on getting through lines quickly and wasn't the slightest bit happy about the prospect of holding anyone up. So when this person threw me a bone ("Would you like me to help you with that?") I jumped on it ("Hell, yes," I said, "otherwise it's gonna be dark by the time I get this thing open"). I'd been feeling more and more at ease in this person's presence even though I wasn't at all sure they were any more comfortable in mine, but after we'd both had a laugh at my expense, it felt very comfortable between us. I'm back to only going into the CVS occasionally, but I'm always grateful to see that familiar face.

A little while back, the hosts over at Radiolab did this mind-blowing series called *Gonads*.[51] It really should be listened to in its entirety—there's a lot of cool stuff throughout—but here's a quick sum-up of what I consider to be the most mind-blowing segment. The one about the bluehead wrasse fish.

Now, if you happen to be born a male bluehead wrasse, life's looking pretty good. You've got your own personal harem swimming around with you, and you get to mate with them every day—repeatedly—due in large part to possessing a distinctive set of black and white stripes (the Oreo) that the ladies find irresistible. As mating consists of releasing sperm into the water at the same time a female is releasing eggs, this might not be all that it's cracked up to be, but nonetheless a sweet-sounding set-up.

There's a problem with only having one male in the group, however, and it's a big one. What happens if the male is eaten by a predator? The whole harem becomes infertile—instantly—and there goes the gene pool.

But nature, in her infinite wisdom, has a solution. Because within a very short period of time, one of those female fish

---

[51] https://www.wnycstudios.org/podcasts/radiolab/projects/radiolab-presents-gonads Gonads: X&Y begins at 27:46

(the largest, apparently) starts to get a little flirty, a little frisky with the other females. And before you know it, she's getting even bigger, her markers begin to change, and then her ovaries begin to . . . keep holding your breath. . . *disintegrate.* By this point you can probably guess what's coming next; she soon starts making sperm and sure enough we've got our old harem back with one male again. Fuck all the way off, right? But it turns out this isn't even a fluky situation. There's a list of other fishes who demonstrate the same behavior. And not only other fish, but some mammals too. So you can either believe there's some transgender activist behind all this, or you can accept that gender is more complicated than you might have otherwise thought.

The fact that humans can approximate much of this transformation with hormones (or surgery) is similarly a lot to take in. As a guy, you tend to go with your instincts, that your masculinity is immutable, unshakeable. And, as I said before, there's a way that it really does feel like a part of who you are. But there's a limit to how deeply this feeling can go, and that seems to unsettle some men. I know it unsettled me when I first contemplated the idea that no matter how butch I might be feeling when I got up on a given morning, I was in fact just a weekly shot away from boobs. Or realizing that girl I grew up with was now sporting facial hair and bigger muscles and might soon be out-wrestling me on the mat.

People changing between genders, or people who express characteristics of both genders, or people who aren't comfortable being labelled as either gender, give the lie to the idea that gender is something as simple as a box to be checked on a form. And they also give the lie to any kind of regimented sexuality in those who are attracted to them.

If you're a female who happens to be in love with someone who's transitioning from male to female, is it on, what, day sixty-three of their hormone treatment that you go from being straight to gay? I'm not aware of having met any hermaphrodites, but if I did get together with such a person, what would I be expected to do, take an inventory of their parts to see whether I was having more of a homosexual or heterosexual experience? And even if my partner simply refuses to identity as male or female, exhibiting characteristics of both, where does that leave my orientation? Does anyone else really have the power to determine my own sexual identity?

It's confusing, right? I'm still a little confused and I'm the one writing about this stuff. But I've spent (way too much) time trying to think it all through, and I've got some additional ideas. Advice even. Some of it's bound to get a little preachy so if you're not into soapboxers, you could gracefully exit here.

IV. RECOMMENDATIONS

Every once in a while, I'd lock in with someone I'd just slept with. Knowing that, sure, we'd be getting back to our lives soon enough, but not feeling the urge to go anywhere right away. The street noise outside the window would stay muted and the light slanting through the blinds would seem to come from so far away, and for whatever reason, I felt like holding on a little longer.

The guy I happened to be with had his head tucked slightly under my armpit, his arm wrapped around me just tight enough to suggest he thought I might be able to protect him from something. Not a feeling I was unused to, but maybe a little odd in this case, because when the door had opened twenty minutes earlier, he'd given off more than a little gangbanger vibe. Oversized hoodie, baggy warmups. His voice wasn't gruff; he'd barely used it beyond tossing off a few syllables for greeting purposes, but you only needed to hear one of them to catch the Borough accent. When the hoodie came off, which was almost immediately, I saw he wasn't overly muscled, just tight everywhere, nothing wasted. We'd been lying on the mattress like that for a while when he broke the silence.

"You like me?" he asked, propping himself up for the moment.

I looked at him. It had been more a declaration with just the slightest question on the end of it, so I could tell right away it would be easier to handle. Over the years, I'd gotten variations on this type of question from both men and women and I never knew what to do with it. Wasn't the evidence already in? But with him seeming to want to know more about "like" than "Like," and as he was already most of the way there, it didn't seem like any heavy lifting would be required to remove that last bit of doubt. So I nodded.

"Yeah." He nodded back. "You do."

Then he lay back against me, still not completely relaxed but trying to get there. I rubbed his head for a while, and at a certain point he put his hand over mine, not guiding, but following along with the motion of my fingers until, finally, he seemed at ease.

"I don't know, man. I don't think …I'm not sure I'd even be gay if…if it wasn't for …" And he raised his head a bit and flicked his chin downwards. He may have shifted himself, but however it went, I could see what he was getting at. There's an unfortunate medical term for what he was packing, or at least what he was close to packing, but let's just say he had a small pecker, which had gotten overlooked by me in the shuffle. Some guys get hard, some don't; it didn't always stand out or come into play.

"What do you mean?"

"I mean girls won't have nothin' to do with me." His voice was somewhere between frustration and acceptance. I couldn't tell if he was speaking from experience. Still, I felt the need to launch into some lofty spiel. About how it shouldn't matter. Especially not to the right woman. You just have to look around and …

He cut me off early. "You kiddin' me?" And this time he popped his head all the way up, underlining the seriousness of the situation.

Some of his cynicism must have rubbed off on me, because I couldn't help but mention that guys could sometimes be tough to deal with too.

He looked at me, then. With maybe a touch of accusation coming up from the depths of his dark brown eyes, but mostly, I think, gratefulness, and said, "I know that. But guys like you will have me, see?" And he clenched my hand and I clenched his back while trying to figure out who, exactly, guys like me were.

And who were guys like him.

WATCH THE LABELS

Garth Greenwell has it right when he says that "many of us have grown suspicious of monolithic categories—gay, straight … man, woman—and have begun to recognize how inadequate such labels are to encompass the reality of individual lives."[52] Right, that is, if we understand "many of us" to mean "many of us who read the *New Yorker.*"

There are some ideas that come down from on high in the literary/academic world that smack of such disreality, that's it no wonder higher education can get a bad rap with the average person. But Greenwell is a down-to-earth writer who has obviously mixed it up with all sorts of people, and I only wish his thinking would take root in the mainstream culture. Like, yesterday wouldn't be soon enough.

I've used the term "bisexual" up until now because that's what's out there and if you don't start off a conversation using vocabulary people can understand, you're going to have a hard time trying to communicate. But, personally, I find it both too broad and too limiting and it would be enough for me to say I'm simply attracted to all sorts of people in all sorts of ways including sexual ones and leave it at that. Having an explanation for yourself, however, doesn't mean that everyone else is going to accept it. Even Greenwell himself ends his article by saying that despite the pain labels cause, "we may not be able to live without them."

Take, for instance, when a person uses a label *for* themselves that has previously been used *against* them. *Faggot* doesn't have

[52] https://www.newyorker.com/magazine/2019/04/22/the-story-of-a-queer-european-refugee-who-insists-on-self-invention

any concrete meaning besides a bundle of sticks, but it's been used as an insult to convey varying levels of disapproval that may or may not have anything to do with the insulted person's sexuality. If a gay man uses it in reference to himself or his best friend, then the thinking goes he's reclaiming that word for his own purposes, taking some of the sting out of it because now it doesn't have only negative connotations; it's been associated with friendship. What are you going to say to someone who uses a label in this way, or who simply wants to rehabilitate the word "gay" itself by declaiming, "I'm *proudly* gay"? You're gonna say, "Good on ya" and move on.[53]

Next up. I'm not saying there aren't a bunch of people out there who are, for all intents and purposes, gay or straight. There are all sorts of people out there. But I am going to suggest there's a way that the categories we use to define people don't fully exist, or if they do, exist mostly in our minds, and it's a risk to equate your individual self with such a category since it's not possible for your life experience to match up perfectly with anyone else's. (In the same sense that there aren't really "Americans," only people who live in America; the concept could mean something equally strong but different to a young person whose parents just migrated here, to one who can trace her lineage back to the

---

[53] For now, anyway. Planted within this pride are the seeds for "I'm proudly straight." And then you realize how one is saying I'm proud of having sex with a human creature and the other is saying I'm proud of having sex with a slightly different looking human creature and it's hard, ultimately, to appreciate the sense of accomplishment that goes along with either. The reason that proudly straight sounds so ridiculous is because that's pretty much all it has going for it, whereas the proudly gay person is reacting against a long history of bigotry and what they're really saying is, "I've got nothing to be ashamed of."

Mayflower or the *Henrietta Marie*, to a Native son whose roots go back thousands of years.)

Labels offer such precious little information about a person, and what they do give is often overwhelmed by stereotypes surrounding that label. If you want to think of yourself as an American, fine, but the more interesting question to ask is *how* are you American. *How* are you straight? *How* are you gay? Because there's an obvious way a guy with a husband and kids attending weekly worship has more in common with the Browns down the street than with his friend who's hitting up the bathhouses every weekend (who himself is more like their third buddy who keeps a barstool with his name on it at Hooters). It's like, okay, you're straight. Now what?

And even focusing exclusively on a person's sexual experience or projected sexual experience finds differences. "I'm straight" is slightly different from "I've only slept with women and I expect I only ever will sleep with women." And "I'm gay" is slightly different from "I slept with a couple women, but it felt like something was missing and I've been with guys ever since."

These are cumbersome, I'll admit; it's easier to say, I'm straight or gay. But that's not the only issue. There are people out there who might be willing to try a similar description of themselves rather than the label—one that actually says something about a person, their history as an individual rather than referring to a more amorphous category—but then feel forced back into using a label because of public reaction. Where the "expect" in "I expect I'll only ever sleep with women" is intentionally trying to leave a bit of wiggle room but the consequence of doing so is having a bunch of guys lined up outside your door wondering if they can change your mind. Or "I slept with a couple women" means your next-door neighbor won't stop harassing you every time her niece comes to visit. About how the two of you should have dinner together. About what a nice couple you'd make. (He *says* he's been with women in the past. He could do it again . . . and he's *so cute.*) Here, who can blame you for wanting to say, "Could you back off, Mrs. Markley? I'm gay, all right?"

But that's a lot easier to understand when you're the one labeling yourself.

A woman recently wrote into a panel of advice columnists on *Slate*[54], a little freaked out after spending the weekend with her husband and a group of his old college friends—and finding out he used to have sex with his best buddy both during and after college. She felt betrayed he'd never told her about it and worried about the implications. To wit, "I am now wondering what else he is hiding from me and exactly 'when' this sexual relationship stopped, or dare I say, if it has stopped at all."

The commentators do an amazingly competent job of trying to talk the wife down, sympathizing with her reaction without ever giving in to it. One laments, "There still exists the idea that if a guy has had sex with one other guy, he must be gay." Another adds, "It's giving me a throwback vibe to the late '90s when it felt like everyone was telling people to pick a side."

If only it were a throwback.

Because in this same online magazine, less than two months previously, you can find another inquiry to a different advice columnist (they've got a lot of advice columnists, apparently) from some parents who found their son "fooling around in

---

[54] https://slate.com/human-interest/2019/12/husband-best-friend-sex-kept-secret-advice.html

a hot tub one night" with a male friend.[55] The parents are wondering what to do about it, and even though the advice is warm, thoughtful, and in almost every other way helpful, it includes the line, "I can't tell you why [your son] hasn't told you yet that he's gay." And what I'm thinking is, *Maybe that's because he's not.* And by going with that baseline assumption, by assuming he's picked a side, all the good intentions both the parents and the advice columnist share in terms of wanting to support this young man are possibly lost by not simply addressing the situation as it came in over the wire.

I agree with the columnist that it would be better not to confront him about what happened, but let's say those parents do get that opportunity. A few mornings later at the breakfast table the kid goes, "Hey, I know Dad saw me and Ben in the hot tub the other night. You guys have any problem with that?" The best answer if you can muster it: "None." Full stop. Then, if you've got some bonus material to add, you could throw out a line like "Ben seems like a great guy," or "We always hear you two laughing together." (Or conversely, "I hear Ben smokes a lot of weed" and you could take the discussion in another direction.) But telling him you've joined a support group for parents of gay teens in the intervening seventy-two hours, or that if he ever wants to tell you he's gay he should know you'll never stop loving him, could unnecessarily muddy the waters. Potentially putting your son in a position of having to defend or explain his sexuality, which he might not yet understand himself. It could still go a bunch of different ways and you should remain open to all the possibilities. Taking your lead from your son, who, if

[55] https://slate.com/human-interest/2019/10/when-son-is-gay-care-and-feeding.html

not right at that moment, then at some point in the future, will know better than anyone what direction to follow.

Taken together, these advice columnists represent the dueling impulses that are in all of us with respect to labels. Trying not to use them, and yet continually tempted to do so. Even the cutting-edge panel investigating the Case of the Questionable Husband can't resist getting tangled up with labels, and when you do that, it's hard to come out unscathed. Here are some more thoughts from one of the panelists concerning the husband's special relationship with his best friend:

1. "Four years of hookups with one other guy does not a homosexual make." (True-ish but then what makes a "real" homosexual; what was this guy when he was in bed with his best friend?)
2. "He might even be totally hetero aside from [this relationship]." (Sure, the husband might otherwise have only been into women, but it's hard to process the idea of him being *totally* hetero except for all those times when he *totally* wasn't?)
3. And, "Bisexual people are perfectly capable of committing to a single person of one gender, if he is in fact roughly there in the spectrum."

Aside from giving a shout out to the point about bisexuals being able to commit, I want to double down on the reticence the writer has in even putting the husband in the bisexual category. Bisexuality is not a single point on the spectrum, nor does it represent some mysterious third side. At its worst, the term can become a dumping ground for a bunch of different sexualities that people don't know what to do with: The guy who enjoyed his MMF three-way with a co-worker of his girlfriend, but did it primarily to please his girlfriend, along with the guy who enjoyed his MMF three-way after having suggested the idea himself with one of his own co-workers in mind.

People have tried to accommodate this diversity by moving beyond the bisexual label and coming up with more expansive ways to describe themselves (polysexual, pansexual, omnisexual), or broadening the definition of straight (hetero-flexible), or introducing other terms (sapiosexual, demisexual) when they don't feel like their desires are being adequately captured by what's out there. But if we're going to stick all these newer labels together and relegate them to a plus sign (LGBT+), or keep adding letters to the acronym until we run out of alphabet (LGBTPPOHSD), or use a sometimes-slur like Queer to round out LGBTQ (LGTBQ, where the Q can also stand for Questioning), maybe we could first highlight what they all have in common by offering anyone who was interested an S for simply being Sexual, no matter who they might want to be—or felt themselves capable of being—sexual with. [56]

If you're Sexual, even if the vast majority of sexual situations you find yourself in are with one type of person, you don't need to fret when something comes up that doesn't fit your normal routine. You don't need to worry about that time you went backpacking around Portugal and the unexpected same-sex encounter you had there. You don't need to worry if you've been with guys your whole life and suddenly find yourself in a sexual relationship with a woman who initially just wanted

[56] As transgender is not an orientation, the T gets to stand above the fray.

you to be the father of her child. And you don't need to worry about whether sleeping with that gender fluid individual made you feel more homosexual or heterosexual (or ceterosexual) since you were just *being sexual* when you were with that person and you're covered.

Being sexual is the only description that makes any real sense anyway, no matter whose sexuality you're referring to, and I think we instinctually realize this with the way we talk about these things. Let's say you stop by Tom's apartment and you ask him where Dick is and he says, "Aw, he's in the bedroom messing around with Harry." He's not likely to tell you, "Aw, he's in the bedroom *being gay* with Harry." And it's a good thing because we kind of think we know what that means, but what does it mean really? Much less than the simple statement of fact explaining the messing around. And that's certainly at least as true if Harry happens to be in the bedroom messing around with Dick and Jane. Because as I've taken great pains to point out, no bisexual has any actual bisexual moments in their life, just sexual moments, and as life is just a series of moments, it's hard to pin down exactly where this so-called bisexuality is happening.

I was in one of those rowboats in Central Park with two friends: the woman I'd known for years and the guy she'd known for years, and while it's true we were all out on the water in minimal clothing, there'd been little indication that day of anything but camaraderie between us. Laughs. Liquid refreshment. Light conversation with the occasional thought-provoker. All of us just sharing a beautiful afternoon in New York. At a certain point we'd taken a break from paddling and were just kicking back when I noticed I had a bit of a situation going on. "Sorry," I said, "y'all are gonna have to excuse me for a sec," and I rolled off the side of the boat to chill things out. Just after that, I heard another splash and realized the guy had jumped in the water, too. He swam over to me and said, "The same thing was happening to me, dude. I don't know what that was all about." I didn't really know either. I mean, I could attempt some rough calculation about who or what was turning me on, but it would be extremely rough. It was both of them, it was neither of them, it was the sun on my crotch. What label would've been of any use to us here? It had become, briefly, a sexual *situation*. And anyone of any purported sexuality has the potential to both contribute to and draw off that (the woman affirmed as much after giggling at us from the boat).

Referring to yourself as sexual isn't really labeling yourself at all. It's a factual description of how you're feeling at any given moment. One that can be measured physiologically, in men and women and everyone in between. If you're sexual, you're going to be open to a variety of sexual experiences, possibly with more than one gender, and if you're not, you're going to be open to none.[57]

Look, this could just be wishful thinking, but there's a chance that most people or at least many people are sexual first before they're anything else. I just don't feel the need to distinguish myself any further from that sentiment and I've got a pretty deep instinct that says I shouldn't have to be the one

[57] I presume the longer you go without having sexual feelings, the more likely you'd be to call yourself asexual, making the difference between an asexual person and a sexual one the standout dichotomy I see in all of this sexuality business.

with a label. But I've got an even deeper one that says I shouldn't be telling people how they should be describing themselves, so to bottom-line all of this:

When should you use labels? For yourself, whenever you want.

When should you avoid them? Whenever you can.

TEACH YOUR TEENS

The sex-related talks we had with our kids over the years were pretty routine. (*This is why mommy's breasts look different from yours. Here's a banana, here's a condom, now watch carefully. It's totally cool to diddle yourself, just please not at the dinner table.)* But the one talk that I considered most important wasn't about private parts or the mechanics of sex at all. That type of information is so readily available to any young person now, anyway, and even if your child isn't particularly adept with the search bar, then surely one of her friends is (meaning that for the first time in history, that equally inexperienced friend might actually know what she's talking about).

The topic I was most concerned with was subtler and it had to do with consent; the captive audience in this case being our middle boy, a sophomore in high school at the time. I didn't feel like I needed to get into the signs of how to tell when someone likes you—he was still young enough that the information could, and had been, passed along the gossip chain—so I launched into the more serious material about what happens next, how far things go, and comfort levels around that. I began with getting him to think about his own. Mentioning there could be times he might not be comfortable with something intimate and he shouldn't feel weird backing off. That this needn't say anything more about him besides his being a cautious person, which he generally is, but that he didn't need a reason to feel hesitant. All he needed was the simple awareness that he might be uncomfortable and try not to get in over his head.

Awareness was really the whole point of the discussion, anyway, my wanting him to just pay attention, not something teenagers are always known for doing. We talked about what it might look like if he started kissing someone, say, and he took a moment to step outside himself and tap into how the other person was feeling. That seemed like a reasonable ask to him. And then, for the kicker, I told him no matter what he thought he'd sussed out, he should take a moment to pause. Stop. To see if the other person came back at him. And if they didn't, not to start up again.

I wondered if he'd complain that was too tall an order to fill, and I'd been prepared to tell him, *well, too damn bad*, but on the fly, I thought of a way to maybe settle the matter and added quickly, "You think you'd have any problem bringing things to a screeching halt if parents walked in?" He laughed and shook his head back and forth in a big way. No, it wouldn't be a problem. I finished that segment by pointing out that if he had a buzz on, he'd probably feel even less like he needed to do this, but that was the exact time he needed to make sure that he did.[58]

I didn't want to rain on his sex-parade because physical contact with another person can be one of life's finer things, but I made clear it just wasn't worth it without a little consideration attached because the consequences could be so far-reaching for everyone involved. I wasn't telling him to pull himself out of the moment, but rather asking him to go more deeply into it. A good habit to get into, anyway, and one that shouldn't cause him to have to overthink every moment, every time, because I pointed out, once you have a partner, you'll learn to understand each other's rhythms better and have a better chance of knowing when and if they're in the mood before you even have to think about it. The time to pay extra attention, I said, was with a new person, or when trying something new with a not so new person.

I used gender neutral pronouns throughout our discussion—you can be sure I didn't want to make any assumptions about his sexuality—but for that reason I wasn't comfortable talking about same-sex experiences, either, or sharing anything about my own (read the book, kid). He'd shown an interest in girls, had given me no cause to bring it up, but I realized later I could've put a finer point on the reason behind "stop and see

[58] The boy's school ended up showing a little stick figure cartoon video on the subject that was better than my talk. It compared wanting to have sex with someone to offering them a cup of tea, and then ran that analogy to the ends of the earth. I.e., just because someone wanted tea on Friday, doesn't mean they'll want it again on Monday. Someone can ask for tea and then at any point when you're in the process of making that tea change their mind and decide they don't want it after all. And no, you definitely don't take the liberty of pouring tea down someone's throat when they're not fully conscious. https://www.youtube.com/watch?v=pZwvrxVavn-Q&feature=emb_logo

if they come back at you"—*because people may respond to you physically for a number of different reasons but none of them might be because they're really into it*—and I could have done it without mentioning anything to do with gender. Or my past.

There are a lot of ways a sexual encounter can go wrong, but almost all the serious ones come about as the result of two people coming from different places, with the person not anticipating the encounter bearing the brunt of it every time. It's a lot more straightforward if someone makes a move on you and you quickly make it clear either verbally or physically or both, *No way, Jose,* and it ends there. That doesn't mean you're not going to be flustered afterwards, that doesn't mean a wrench isn't going to get thrown into that relationship, but at least you've got a chance of moving on with your life as more or less the same person as you were before.

But it's not as clear-cut when someone you're friends with, someone you respect, makes a move on you and you don't stop it right away (or don't stop it at all). Assuming you're not feeling good about it, you're already in a lot of trouble right there, and then if you add in the same-sex feature you've got an additional complication. You could be in a kind of shock, and then if you're a guy and realize at some point your dick's gone hard that's going to compound the shock. And the thing is, a lot of guys' dicks are going to get hard in a lot of sexual situations, so if you're really attached to your sexual identity, then you're bound to struggle trying to put it back together the way it was before.[59]

This is how I felt about it, anyway, after the prep school buddy incident.

I didn't know about any studies, I hadn't read any books, and I wasn't able to google "What does it mean when I thought I was straight and then_______" —and see that a bunch of other people had asked the same question, filling in the blank with similarly related material. The issues I should've been trying to get my head around from that night— "Was my relationship with this guy ever what I thought it was?" and "Did the trust I'd built up in him over years just crumble in a matter of minutes?" and "Did he let me down more by starting it than I let him down by ending it?"—got pushed aside by *My dick sure didn't seem to have any problem being in my friend's mouth* and *I can't say I did anything when he subsequently pulled himself out and stuck his crotch in my face besides return the favor* and even *Maybe*

[59] To cite perhaps the most famous study on the subject, conducted with 1) a group of self-identified straight males (who were further categorized as homophobic or non-homophobic), 2) gay porn, and 3) a penile plethysmograph machine which measured the reaction of the first to the second: thirty-four percent of the non-homophobic group had a measurable reaction along with eighty percent of the homophobic group. You can draw your own conclusions about what that might say about homophobic men, but if you accept increasing circumference of the penis as way to measure arousal, then the larger point is that a bunch of self-identified straight guys responded to gay porn. The study has been called problematic in a number of ways but let's just throw it out there as one way to try to take the temperature of the situation. Adams, Henry E. et al. "Is Homophobia Associated with Homosexual Arousal?" Journal of Abnormal Psychology, Vol. 105, No. 3, pages 440-445, 1996. https://www.psychologytoday.com/files/u47/Henry_et_al.pdf

this whole thing could've been avoided if I'd just been wearing some bedclothes. I believe I was reading on top of the covers when he came down, for the last time truly unselfconscious being in my underwear around friends. Every thought focused on my actions—not his—even though it felt forced enough that I refused to even think about some of the details afterward because of their complicated implications. The conclusion: *I guess I really must have liked it, or I would've stopped things right away; my responsibility, my bad.*

It took a while for me to be able to make a connection between what happened that night and my, uh, distaste for giving head. I remember well walking out of an early client's house, happy with the cash in my pocket but, before I'd even hopped on my motorcycle, telling myself "I'm gonna fuck the next guy so good he's never gonna have a chance to even *think* about getting his dick near my face." To my boyfriend, "I don't know, I guess I've got a pretty bad gag reflex." And, in general, *A penis is just an overgrown clitoris that's been bathed in a different amount of hormones, why should this be such an ordeal?* But it was an ordeal, and remained yet another casualty of an unresolved evening.

Without being able to talk to the other person to try to come to some kind of understanding, without being able to put something like this in context, you've got few good options. You can hate on yourself (I did initially). You can become an extreme homophobe (I probably would've if I'd managed to sustain that self-hatred). Or you can stay in a kind of purgatory between non-acceptance and acceptance (where I remained for a while, leaving my personal level of homophobia about where it'd been before). You can decide that if you weren't already gay before, you are now (I tried that on for size right afterwards, and then again later). Or you can keep going down the list, hoping that something will click that makes sense.

My sexuality seems so fundamental to me now that it's hard to believe it once looked very different. The fact that I came to see sleeping with other guys as just not a big deal, as merely another way of expressing myself around like-minded men, seems not just essential to my being, but to my well-being. And without this experience, I'm not sure I would've turned out the same. Can I imagine other scenarios that would've led me to a similar place without leaving such a bad taste in my mouth? Ones where I didn't feel ambushed, where I had a chance to be a fully willing participant. Of course. But I can imagine plenty of worse ones, too, and I keep coming back to the fact that I'm not sure I would've been open to any later opportunity without first *knowing* I was up for it. Because despite the smattering of things I mentioned in the Qualifications section, beyond a high school dream, I simply hadn't entertained any fantasies about guys and I'm just not sure those things would've—on their own—left enough of an impression for me to explore further. Even at twenty-seven when I had an incentive to try to explain my behavior with women, I'm thinking I might well have gone on being an asshole, hoping I'd outgrow it. And that makes relying on some other random situation to have cropped up and made me the person I am today a dicey proposition.

If the choice, then, is between this happening and nothing at all, then it's better that it happened. But the fact that I choose to put the experience in a more positive light in no way implies a recommendation that anyone else in a similar situation should do the same. Because regardless of how I came to view it, this box is not one that everyone wants opened. Same-sex attraction remains a charged issue. And until the day when it no longer is, it's a box that should be handled with special care.

So if you're thinking about making a same-sex move on someone whose sexuality you're not sure about (or, obviously, any move on anyone whose interest you're not sure about), my advice shouldn't come as a surprise. Don't. Later in life, I made this mistake by trying to kiss someone who I thought wanted me to and didn't (although I also made the mistake of not making a move on someone who I later found out wished I had, so look, you can't call them all). But it's a great area to put on your conservative hat and be conservative. If you're older, if you're the known quantity sexuality wise, and the other person isn't, then let that person make the first move or be the one to put out a flashing neon signal. Because sometimes shy is just a way of saying you're not ready for something.

I'm glad I didn't mess around with any of my friends back in high school. There is definitely some power in knowing you could've but didn't. Knowing that you can but don't. Not that I had access to this kind of knowledge back then but, in retrospect, I can see all the hidden benefits we got from having that implicit boundary in place. Because one of the best things about platonic relationships is . . . they're platonic. And the more people I slept with, the more I began to value the people close to me who I hadn't.

I wish when I was younger, on a couple of nights at least, a buddy and I might have jerked off together rather than getting stupidly drunk (simply getting drunk with no action would've been fine, I'm talking about blotto). At the point in the night when we were pretty gone but still functioning. When we knew nothing else interesting was likely to happen, our girlfriends were busy, or gone home, or we were in a fight with our girlfriends, or we were between girlfriends, I wish we'd just fucked around. To show we didn't give a shit, yes, but mostly just to have a change of pace, and maybe even a better night in the end. Because we weren't going to sleep and the only option seemed to have been more drinks, which is what we always had. And there's a point where more drinks are always stupid (the older you get the sooner this point comes).

When we were past all the deep talk. Past, for the moment, learning anything new about life or each other. A certain amount of brain cells lost, sure, but plenty of others that could still be saved! Before the mangled sentences and the preposterous hangover. I say this while knowing my younger self would look at me like I was loose a few screws for mentioning it. I say while knowing full well the risks that would've been involved. And I say this without having any particular friend in mind. At the time, I thought about the option with exactly none of them but, looking back, any one of them might have done.

What's the point of those two contradictory messages? They're the two angles I would share if a younger person was trying to make up their minds about something like this and happened to ask my advice. I certainly wouldn't tell them to cross the line. And I wouldn't tell them not to cross it. I'd tell them to think on it. Are you able to test the waters by sticking a toe in? Can you be savvy about dropping hints, and picking up hints, and most importantly, notice when a dropped hint hasn't been picked up? And if that hint isn't picked up, are you prepared to be more grateful than disappointed that you were able to get this information without getting all wet?

And if the hint is picked up? If your ante is met or even raised? Realize that even though you're both on board sailing into it, you might not come out the same on the other side. One of you might have more of a hang-up about it afterward and take it out on the friendship. And even if you both make it through without hang-ups, but with one of you wanting to do it again and one of you not, things could get awkward. Messing around introduces a possibility that you never had to seriously consider before and now you might have to always consider it if you find yourselves alone together again at the end of a long night. That can be a drag.

On the other hand, by not doing anything, you might risk the chance of having an even better friendship. Maybe your friendship is the type that can not only handle it, but will strengthen as a result. Maybe you're both low-key enough that you can keep it low-key. That neither of you are the type to push each other. That you can let what happened sink back into the depths of the friendship and if it resurfaces again for both of you, great, and if it doesn't, just as great. That's a lot to ask but it can be done. I've done it. With men and with women.[60]

KNOW THE FACTS

When I was younger, I accepted without hesitation that homosexuality was an aberration among humans because it was never found in the larger animal kingdom. Not like anyone ever gave me a formal presentation on the subject, but from

[60] As to what to tell anyone else about what you did or didn't do with your friend, I'd say, "Keep 'em guessing."

information I picked up here and there it seemed that all species got together in monogamous male and female pairs that lived happily ever after like the ones you saw in the Disney cartoons. Not just headliners like *Lady and the Tramp*, but extras, too, like the songbirds in *Snow White*.

And while *aberration* never led to me to conclude *abomination* (most likely because no one close to me had indoctrinated me into such extreme views), I'll admit I had some trepidation at the start of my adventures in San Francisco that I might somehow be going against nature. I wasn't sure what that would feel like, exactly, but to the extent I could check myself against something I didn't know how to measure, I was on the lookout for it during those early encounters. Because I considered nature not only something to be enjoyed and appreciated, but also respected and reckoned with. And this was a fact I couldn't just wish away.

It turns out I didn't have to worry, of course, because researchers have since documented all sorts of "aberrations" in nature, and the idea that sexual activity is limited to monogamous pairs, or occurs only between males and females, or is undertaken purely for procreative purposes has been shown to be more than a bit of a fairy tale. If you were listening close enough, you could actually hear the stripping of the gears in certain quarters as they tried to go from forward to reverse on this. Like, *Homosexuality is disgusting. It's not found anywhere in God's kingdom except among sinful humans. . . Oh wait, it is? Well. What I meant to say is it's disgusting because animals do it. And we're not animals.*

There are two animals that share more genetic material with us humans than any other on the planet. Close to 99%, in fact. And even though bonobos and chimps make up their own genus, it's not a case of if you've seen one ape, you've seen them all, because in the intervening couple million years since they branched off from one another, their approach to life has become quite different.

Here's an opening scene from *Lapham Quarterly* to give you an idea of how those differences look in the wild.

"A bonobo who finds a new fruit tree will report back [to the group], at which point an orgy breaks out, and then after everyone shares in the bounty, another orgy occurs as some kind of digestif. A chimpanzee, on the other hand, might gorge itself on the fruit, guard the tree, and share only with reluctance."[61]

Such opposing behaviors are generally attributed to bonobos having a matriarchal society and chimps a patriarchal one, with the female-dominated bonobos resolving conflicts with sex, while the single alpha male in charge of the chimps maintains order through aggression. By now, the sex lives of bonobos have become legend, and the rich variety has prompted the observation that "the entire species is bisexual."[62] Chimps, meanwhile, are capable of forming strong male-male bonds, but there's not much free love going around between the genders as high-ranking males are known for "monopolizing and guarding the females." Their How to Get a Date playbook includes: pulling out the female's hair, slapping them, beating them, and if all else fails, eating the babies of the female they're interested in, ones

---

[61] https://www.laphamsquarterly.org/animals/our-orgiastic-future?page=all This quotation plus a number of other points from the article are woven in.

[62] https://www.news-medical.net/news/2006/10/23/1500-animal-species-practice-homosexuality.aspx

originally conceived with another male. This forces the female to start a family from scratch, with Mr. Charming figuring he'll now be in a good position to offer his services.[63]

The bonobos are more gender neutral with fewer differences between the sexes, while between male and female chimps there are many. Bonobos mate across communities, chimps avoid their neighbors. Bonobos are known for expressing empathy and kindness to strangers; chimps, well, you get the idea.[64]

So which behaviors sound more human to you?

For years, scientists—the vast majority of them men—focused only on the chimpanzees. In chimp behavior, they found plenty of justification for what were often thought of as the manly attributes: greed, selfishness, aggressiveness, an aptitude for starting wars. Sex was seen as a simple procreative task, a quick in and out before heading off into the jungle with your buddies to hunt, leaving the child rearing (and vacuuming) duties to the females. As paper after paper came in reporting similar results, there was perhaps a collective shrug of the scientists' shoulders. *See, this is just how we are.*

By the time the bonobo connection was discovered and publicized, the chimp story had already gained quite a bit of traction, and consequently, we're still playing catch up. Still, it's hard to believe that some of that early research wouldn't have provoked a concern or two. Humans have generous impulses, too, they have longings for peace, and the researchers must have wondered if there wasn't a missing link. Or at least wished there

---

[63] https://www.livescience.com/48743-aggressive-chimps-reproduce-more.html

[64] https://www.eva.mpg.de/3chimps/files/apes.htm

was one, as bloody conflicts subtract numbers from both sides and when challenges confront the species as a whole, cooperation not just within tribes but among them is essential. Enter the bonobo.

Now you might think I'm all about those hippie bonobos, but I'm not, really. Yes, I have good friends who are genuine hippies (meaning they live off the land, live and let live, and don't wash very much rather than they dropped acid at a concert and think they did the world a favor). And yes, the planet could certainly do with having a few more people like them inhabiting it. But even my friends display the occasionally chimpy characteristic and that's not necessarily a bad thing as there are a number of positive ones to choose from. Chimps are better known for using tools. They can cooperate efficiently in smaller groups. And there's something to be said for having a hierarchical organization in certain circumstances, as orgies—while not without their merits—are unlikely to provide a solution to every problem. More to the point, I'm not a big believer in coincidence, so I can't believe it's coincidental that we've been given both connections and it seems obvious there must be something to be learned from both.

Rather than trying to synthesize our ancestry, however, you can be sure there will be those who will try to pit the cousins against one another in an attempt to figure out who would gain the upper hand. I'm not impervious to this angle, either. In Africa, the bonobos are separated from the chimps by the Congo River but it's not too difficult these days to imagine it drying up. Or, to continue to play anthropomorphologist, to wonder what would happen if a group of chimp-like humans stumbled across a more bonobo-influenced one and threatened their territory. And what I'm thinking is: either you've got to have some decidedly chimp-minded folks in the bonobo group who ultimately support the bonobo cause, or those bonobos better be able to pull off some seriously quick coitus interruptus, and access their inner chimps to be able to defend themselves. Otherwise, it won't matter, anymore, who has the moral high ground. Because there won't be any bonobos left to contest it.

Attacks on members of the LGBTQ community continue to rise in this country, and around the world, people are murdered every day for who they happen to love, or sleep with, or for not presenting their gender in what's considered to be a socially acceptable manner. That would be bad enough, but most of these crimes are committed against an adult population that already represents a reduced number of targets. Because far too many LGBTQ youth have already taken the hint from the culture they were born into and culled themselves out of it in advance.

The Trevor Project rolls out depressing statistics around these harmful behaviors on a regular basis, and perhaps the first thing you're struck with when you look at them is that so many kids of every orientation are having a hard time making it. I can only imagine this sense of despair is coming from that one percent of our DNA that we don't share with our ancestors, as it's generally accepted that humans are the only animals that will try to take their own lives. Still, gay and lesbian youth are having a much harder time—and even though this isn't a contest, and definitely not one you want to win—it's the bisexual-identified kids that consistently, and by large margins, report the greatest feelings of hopelessness, of considering suicide, and of attempting it.[65]

Before she went into private practice, my sister used to be a social worker for at-risk youth. To give me an idea of one of the things she was up to, she showed me a video clip once from a sexuality workshop she'd helped mediate. For the most part, the students self-identified as straight and gay, but there was one guy who was questioning, pulled in both directions. He stood out for a number of reasons: thoughtful, polite, good listener, doing his best to explain his situation, which he didn't like to talk about in public as he felt even less like he fit in there than he did in that room. And yet his reluctance to disclose anything bothered him; he came across as traditionally masculine—in an off-handed rather than heavy-handed way—and there was a sense that the more comfortable he was expressing one of his traits, the more he felt like he was hiding another. Naturally, I found myself rooting for the guy. To figure it all out, to find some peace within himself. But it wasn't too much later that my sister informed me that he'd hanged himself.

Why, dammit? Why would someone who by all reports seemed to be the most well-adjusted kid in the room otherwise, why would he take his own life? I can't pretend to fully understand his situation, but one thing for certain is that he was struggling with his sexuality at the time. That's why you go to a support group. Because you're having trouble handling something on your own.[66]

---

[65] https://www.thetrevorproject.org/2019/03/26/research-brief-bisexual-youth-experience/

[66] I have another example that hits much closer to home, but frankly, I don't know how the guy would feel about my talking about it, and now I'll never get to ask him.

What a shitty reason the world has given someone for thinking about killing themselves. Attraction. I mean, can you imagine, the entire reason that makes life worth living. Attraction to people, places, things, ideas. And in the case of those of us who find ourselves attracted to *more* of the population, how is it possible that could make you feel *less* like you belong? So much less that you give up on trying to fit in entirely.

And it doesn't even have to be that tragic for it to still be pretty darn tragic. Consider the time—precious time, productive time—lost when a young man can't stop stressing about the kiss he just walked away from. The one with a guy he just met at baseball camp *and didn't his dick get hard just the slightest bit quicker than when he was kissing his last girlfriend but he loved kissing his last girlfriend didn't he but maybe he really didn't love it as much as he thought he did so he keeps trying to remember* and ends up sleepwalking through the rest of training instead of perfecting that fastball that was really going somewhere.

Or that young woman. The one so worried that her feelings for her best friend might have just crossed into something sexual the night before *but where was that line exactly between sexual and non-sexual because maybe she was only right up against it but then what was she doing anywhere near it when she'd always only been interested in guys and what does that say about her and what it does it mean going forward and what's gonna happen with the friendship* and on and on and round and round and she could have spent the day starting that extra- credit science project she was going to tackle that semester but now she'd just as soon skip it and settle for the grade she's got.

All that time—wasted—trying to microscopically define your attractions when you should be able to just accept them as they're given. Labels striking you first as useless and then, as you can't help yourself from engaging with them, dangerous. Constantly having to question yourself is exhausting. And the prospect of having to explain yourself to others feels even more daunting.

Personally, I've felt that if I should be writing about anything right now, it should be the climate crisis. Writing about it or getting out and standing shoulder to shoulder with Greta Thunberg and demanding that something be done until it is done. Believe me, I thought about it before undertaking this project, asking myself what's the point of having a bunch of less labeled, more sexually openminded, fully consent-oriented people running around if they're not going to have a sustainable planet to run around on. And yet if that problem, or racial injustice, or inequality are to be overcome, we're going to need all hands on deck, and I don't want to lose any more of them.

CAREFUL WHAT YOU PREACH

There's no single force I can think of that's more responsible for causing people to get twisted up about sexuality than religion and therefore no discussion of sexuality would be complete without mentioning it. So, yeah, I'm going there. This section's not gonna work for any holier than thou secularist who believes religion is for the weak minded, any more than it is for that fundamentalist who can't make any room on their righteous path for the humanist next door, but not to worry, there's only a couple things I want to mention, anyway.

I'm hardly the only one to have this reaction, but it's kind of jaw dropping that you can still tune into a nationally broadcast program and hear someone quoting Bible verses at you as reasons against certain sexual behaviors. And as the Bible is the most commonly used religious handbook in this country, it's the one that makes the most sense to focus on. Not that I'm opposed to quoting verses—from the Bible or any other meaningful text—because I'm a rather big fan of good books and the Bible didn't get the reputation as being the ultimate Good Book for nothing. But I do find it interesting what verses people choose to recite. And at how quickly the commentary about them devolves into a debate about what Leviticus might have meant here, or Paul there, when the response *every single time* should not be to indulge those particular passages any further, but to mention other passages. Like the ones compiled by Valerie Tarico over at *Salon*[67] informing slaves that they should "obey [their] earthly masters with deep respect and fear" (Ephesians 6:5 NLT). That tell a woman, "Everything on which she lies during her menstrual impurity shall be unclean, and everything on which she sits shall be unclean." (Leviticus 15: 19-20) That advise parents their "stubborn and rebellious" sons should be executed by stoning (Deuteronomy 21:18-21). Or show Jesus as grumpy at best when he approaches a fig tree looking for something to eat and, finding the tree barren, proclaims, "May you never bear fruit again!" (causing the tree to immediately wither) (Matthew 21:18-22 NIV). Come on, these don't sound like divinely inspired passages. And if so? I mean, holy shit.

---

67 https://www.salon.com/2014/05/31/11_kinds_of_bible_verses_christians_love_to_ignore_partner/ Tarico provides these as potential remedies to what she refers to as the "anti-queer clobber verses," and she's also responsible for highlighting the positive passage I soon quote about, basically, giving the shirt off your back.

Then when you do get a positive sounding sentiment (of which there are also many), something like, "Anyone who has two shirts should share with the one who has none, and anyone who has food should do the same" (Luke 3:11 NIV), you wonder why *that* advice couldn't be taken literally. There'd be a lot less megachurch mansions and a lot more people with shirts on their back and food in their cupboards. But that's just it, no one follows the Bible literally. Even if they could somehow figure out a way to sort through all the contradictory messages. There are no literalists out there, only selective literalists, and that means what people choose to highlight as God's truth is telling you a lot more about that person than it does about the underlying meaning of a given religious book or, more to the point, God.

I once decided to rewrite all of Jesus's quotations in a notebook to see if I could get a better sense of what He was talking about, and from what I could tell it seemed like His major concerns centered around hypocrisy, care for the poor and oppressed, maintaining a belief in something better, and forgiveness. All admirable principles. Not a single one about sexuality. And since then, these are the passages I have chosen to focus on. Along with any other ones from the Bible, or the Torah, or the Koran, or the Tao Te Ching that emphasize respect and basic morality. Granted, I cherry-pick as much as the next person, but at least I admit it. If you are choosing passages that reflect your own fears, then surely you're only picking the rotten fruit.

I've got nothing against religious people. I am a religious person. And the God that reveals itself to me is a loving God. I've felt that love countless times in my life, as many times, approximately, as I've felt unworthy of it. But that's exactly where the rub is: Feeling that no matter how poorly you've acted, or how awful things may seem, that there's still something good about you and the world that you live in. And even though my sense of what "good" might mean has broadened over the years, what hasn't changed is the belief that I'm most connected to God when I'm treating other people well, and furthest from God when I'm not.

It just doesn't seem right that the countries where religion is considered such an important influence in people's day to day lives are generally the worst in their treatment of their LGBTQ citizens, while the ones that treat their LGBTQ citizens the best are the least religious.[68] And it just doesn't seem fair that religious faith should be linked *to* suicidal behavior in LGBTQ young adults. Having a sense that there's some larger purpose, that it's not just all "whatever," should be protective *against* suicide. And it is. In heterosexual-identified young adults only.[69] And while I certainly don't think you need a relationship with God to live a good life and make it through this world, I can't accept that having one should make it harder to do so.

"Religion" isn't even really the problem, anyway. It's these seemingly false prophets who end up behind the pulpit instead of taking their places humbly in the pew, spewing an ideology

68 https://en.wikipedia.org/wiki/Importance_of_religion_by_country https://www.asherfergusson.com/lgbtq-travel-safety/ The twenty worst countries in terms of LGBTQ rights report, on average, being 93% religious, while the twenty best ones report less than half that percentage of religiosity. South Africa, at least when it comes to legal rights, is a rare exception.

69 https://www.reuters.com/article/us-health-lgbq-religion-suicide/religious-faith-linked-to-suicidal-behavior-in-lgbq-adults-idUSKBN1HK2MA

that we have to fight our way out from under rather than one that supports us. We shouldn't have to keep reminding ourselves that these were the bodies we were born into, there isn't anything disgraceful about them. That it's an eye for an eye that makes the whole world blind, not masturbation. That our attractions are God-given.

V. BACKGROUND CHECK

There were concerns my mother would be going to hell, and hoping to avoid this debacle, her great-aunts whisked her from her crib, bundled her up, and snuck her off to be re-baptized, this time Catholic. My mother's grandmother had grown up on the banks of the River Shannon in Ireland, and even though she'd raised her sister's eyebrows by marrying a Protestant of Scottish and English stock, her Catholicism had prevailed through another generation. Until one of those offspring—my grandmother—strayed further from the fold and married a Baptist.

My maternal grandfather's history was less complicated, but not without its quirks. His family hailed from the long-contested Alsace-Lorraine region—French flag flying over it one year, German the next—and this helped to explain the pairing of his German sounding first name, Fritz, with his French sounding last one. Faced with disparate backgrounds, my grandfather and grandmother threw up their hands and decided to raise my mother and uncle Presbyterian.

On my father's side, at least, everyone was Jewish. But they were far flung Jews, my grandfather's parents born in Poland and Austria, my grandmother's Russia. At eighteen, my great-grandmother set sail for New York with the tailor she'd fallen in love with, never to see her parents again. Along with her, she'd taken her youngest brother Jack, and when my birth followed his death many decades later, I was named after him.

I am, in my own way, an American. And it was never going to work out real well for me to imagine the damnation of one side of my family based on where they'd come from, or the eternal damnation of the other because of what faith they practiced. Long before I started working through my views on sexuality, I had to make sense of my history, and I can see now how one informed the other.

My relatives are all decent, hardworking people. They respect one another. And their differing beliefs in the divine strengthen their backs in much the same way. Should I tell the Christians to become Jews, the Jews Christians? Do I wish they'd all join the Unitarian Church I attend that will take in pretty much anybody, regardless of belief? None of the above. I appreciate them as they are.

And it's not so different when it comes to sexuality or gender. I'm not interested in a world where everyone is androgynous or sexually fluid any more than I am in a world where everyone is expected to choose a side—to be this or that. Some people feel their sexuality or gender so strongly that it might as well be a religion. A woman who treasures her Womanhood and all the thrills and frills that go along with it. Or a guy who says his heart will only go pitter- patter for another guy. Straight, male, not so straight, not so male. There's room for all of it. It shouldn't have to be a choice between erasing the lines that can exist between people and erasing the people who straddle the lines. Or choose, at times, not to recognize them at all.

AUTHOR NOTES

Most all of the Americans' names have been changed (exceptions include Kiki, of course, we're not changing Kiki).

"Our boys" refers to the two fine boys that came with my (now former) partner. I raised them like sons, but they've got a great dad who was gracious enough to let me share in their raising for many years and, in fact, the banana and condom demonstration I reference is one he told me about over a beer.

"Recently" generally refers to any time in the last couple of years, which is roughly the amount of time I've been working on the book. Time stamps are a royal pain as they are constantly shifting out from under you, but for the most part I'm sticking with the originals as they were accurate when I wrote them.

Finally, it should be understood that there's this book, and then there's the much crappier version that would've existed without the help of Rachel Stout, Patrick Price, and Jessica Kubzansky. Thank you, also, to Paula Munier for motivating me to get organized, and to Hitch for being Hitch.

www.ingramcontent.com/pod-product-compliance
Lightning Source LLC
LaVergne TN
LVHW091302150826
845673LV00006B/1507

* 9 7 9 8 9 8 5 6 9 7 2 0 9 *